The Garden

Theology

Discovering Design
Acquiring Identity

Jan H. Lamprecht

DEDICATION

*To all the seekers out there
who turned out not to be slaves,
but offspring.*

ACKNOWLEDGEMENTS

My wife, Han-Mari, for temporarily ceasing to invent chores for me to execute, thereby allowing me to focus on finishing this project. The more I survey the dynamics of Jesus' love for His bride, the more I love you!

My local church family, Pro Gratia Malmesbury and everyone at Dynamic Love Ministries.

Cover art and concept by:
Chris Alford at Chris Alford Graphic Design
www.chrisalford.com

Photography in cover art courtesy of:
Harold Head
www.haroldhead.com

Author portrait photo by:
DLM Studios

CONTENTS

ABOUT THE AUTHOR

Born in the winter of 1978 in the old Transvaal and growing up in the corn-capital of South Africa in the Free-State, Jan Hendrik Lamprecht always felt the call of God on his life. On leaving school he enrolled in the MAP (Mission Apprentice Program) presented by World Missions, at Immanuel World Mission School in the Free-State. Later he enrolled for a correspondence course in theology through ICI, but unfortunately that didn't work out as planned and he didn't complete the course.

Jan Lamprecht and his wife, Han-Mari, currently reside in Malmesbury in the Swartland region of the Western Cape where he works as a self-employed plumber. They are members of Pro Gratia Malmesbury. His passion for the gospel was rekindled on hearing the good news preached in a way he had never heard it preached before. He is currently enrolled in the DLM discipleship course.

FOREWORD

Some years ago we wanted to renovate our bathroom. We got some plumbers in to quote on the job. Jan was one of them. We started to talk about Jesus that day and we have not stopped ever since.

Jan is a man that loves truth and want to understand why things are the way they are. He finds the power of life in the explanation of the *"why"*. Why did God make us? Why did Jesus have to die? Why a resurrection? Why a garden? What was this garden, what is sin, what is forgiveness, what is innocence..? This makes me think of the following passage:

"But he that received seed into the good ground is he that hears the word, and understands it; which also bears fruit, and brings forth, some a hundredfold, some sixty, some thirty." Matthew 13:23

Fruit bearing is found in understanding the word of God, which is the message that Jesus portrayed to the world. *The Garden Theology* is many years of walking with God in the quest to understand these concepts placed in a short, yet thought provoking, as well as explanatory writing that will enrich the reader.

What I love about the book is the simplicity in which very complex concepts are explained, prompting you to go and do deeper study in the Word of God as well as digging deep into yourself to live the true meaning God has given to life.

The beauty of *The Garden Theology* is that it is the fruit of the Holy Spirit through an ordinary man, with an ordinary job, put in words in such a way that you cannot put what he says in a theological box of what has already been heard and known. The relationship based approach of a God whose desire is to walk with man, and would never abandon His original plan, is the foundation of this writing and will bless every person that reads it.

As you read this book make sure you prepare your heart to be challenged by a different logic than the traditional law based system that has brought many into bondage. Every sub-chapter is concise and to the point. You will not be bored by long theological reasoning that never comes to a conclusion. Jan, true to himself simply says it as it is when he clearly explains what grace is and what it is not.

This book will bring a good framework of what the Gospel is in its essence, bringing understanding that will lead to a fruit filled life of grace. I am grateful that these truths can be placed in one book that is an easy read and simple to understand.

Be ready to think differently about who God is, why you are here and how this Kingdom operates.

- Bertie Brits
  Author of: *Born from Innocence* & *Jesus is the Tithe.*
  Dynamic Love Ministries

PREFACE
- A DESIGN CRISIS

What is commonly diagnosed in the world and its people, not only in the church, as an identity crisis, that is when people can't seem to find their purpose, is in actual fact a design crisis. Our design somehow evaded us. Or did we circumvent it on account of a different influence? I believe the latter to be true. The serpent in the garden presented man with an alternative design and the rest is history. Regardless what our individual opinions may be, the fact remains, we have been oblivious to our design and that in turn, this caused confusion concerning our identity. We rejected design from pure ignorance and approached identity from a slave mindset and works mentality. As soon as you discover your design, identity follows suit and immediately starts to take shape. Not understanding our design results in the absence of identity. These two go hand in hand and only function on optimal level as a unit.

How often have you heard people say that everyone is made in the image and likeness of God? If that was true most of us who are all too willing to jump on the bandwagon and exclaim *"universalist!"* at a mere statement concerning innocence, would actually also be universalist by this confession that all of mankind already possess His likeness too. His likeness is immortality. His likeness is a constant. If we then say that everyone are already created after His likeness we somehow skipped salvation, that is acquiring our identity by acknowledging our divine design and moved on to immortality. If that's your confession you are way ahead of the rest of us. Please wait up! You will have to wait for immortality. Trust me, you are not alone. As you can see this is a huge generalization brought on by ignorance. It is half a truth, half assumption. Yes, everyone was made in His image. If you are a human being, you are created in His image. His likeness on the other hand is something only Jesus gives and it is slightly more complex than that. Complex, not complicated might I add. Thus I felt the need to write this book.

In this book you will see that being made in His image is not the ultimate, but that the combination of both image and likeness is the ultimate. Let us take a pick-up truck as an example. The pick-up has a certain specification concerning its loading capacity. That does not necessarily mean it is already carrying that load. Loading capacity = image/design and load = identity. Identity in the sense that the pick-up, by way of speaking, acknowledges its design. Its design is for argument's sake 750 kg. When you then utilize its capacity by loading it with 750 kg, you are bringing its identity to the fore and it *"finds"* its purpose. We find our purpose and identity as soon as we see what has already been done for us in Jesus. When we direct our lives according to that truth, the word of God concerning our lives, we start to enjoy His quality of life. But does it stop there? Heavens no! Thats only how it starts off. We have a glorious inheritance when we acknowledge our design. His likeness. So what does His likeness signify then? God's likeness is immortality, also known as eternal life or life in abundance. Under sin we received a wage (death) for our sorrowful labor. In rest we enjoy His quality of life in the here and now. But wait there's more! We have an inheritance. This inheritance is immortality. His quality of life forever in a brand new body, that knows no decay.

The Garden Theology is a grace perspective on the creation, design and identity of mankind. Why the title - The Garden Theology? Simply because God hasn't changed since the creation story and the blue-print for the design and identity of man is exactly the same as it was back then. God placing man in Christ is exactly the same position the first man filled before the fall. This book is about discovering our design, that is, our capacity, our value to the Father and then utilizing our design to *"carry"* His identity. When God stoops down to us in the incarnation of Jesus in human flesh, He not only shows us what to believe about Him, but later in the ascension of Jesus to His right hand, shows us what He ultimately believes about us. God is not waiting for us to conjure up faith. In showing us what He is like, His design, He is actually showing us what we are really like, our design. We change when we see that we are valued. The One we place our trust in becomes our identity. Thus faith becomes inevitable. If we are to discover our design it would probably be a good idea to get to know the designer. It is His image in which we were created after all.

It has been sixteen years since I first heard the good news. I am not saying that I have sixteen years of experience in the gospel of grace, please don't see that as boasting. The reader will soon realize that it's hardly boasting. That is because when I first heard the gospel of grace, I ran away! Prior to hearing the gospel I have been in bible school for five years without knowing anything about God's love for me or how much He valued me. Sad, I know. I was oblivious to the fact that I was the pick-up truck and approached identity from a slave perspective when I was supposed to approach it from a restored image perspective. On the other hand, when you are aware that you are the pick-up truck/new man and know your capacity, it is plain sailing as it is meant to be.

Well, lets get back to that first encounter of grace. An American preacher held a camp meeting type conference in a city about two hours' drive from where I lived at the time. Some pastor fell ill and as a result couldn't attend, so I got invited along in his place all expenses paid. For a student that is like proper provision from God.

I was so overwhelmed by the message of grace that I couldn't even take notes, I was just soaking in all the goodness of the gospel washing over me. Mostly sitting, laughing with my arms hanging beside me. I noticed that my behavior didn't even bother anyone. Sitting there laughing all my cares away was unfortunately short-lived when the preacher said: *"You won't grasp the new life in Christ, unless you see yourself crucified with the Lord on the cross."* Up until recently I became aware that it wasn't his intention to scare me off the gospel, but with my background in the church, being crucified to me meant being humiliated, serving or rather slaving under ungrateful religious leaders so God could look kindly upon me and later reward me for my perseverance. I just wasn't up for that sort of rubbish anymore. I had enough of slaving. I didn't need my nose rubbed in it all over again. Even though I still enjoyed the rest of the camp meeting and the fellowship, my guard was up. I was waiting for someone to elaborate on this being crucified with the Lord stuff. Unfortunately not much was said in connection with the subject. Little did I know that being crucified with Jesus meant that He came to restore God's image in order for us to see in whose image we were made. This guy was speaking *"design"* language and I wasn't aware of it. I couldn't relate because I did not know my design, God's opinion of me. You see the very first thing a new believer needs to know prior to believing is his/her immeasurable value in the eyes of our Father. Knowing this makes it much easier for the individual to relate to a loving God.

On returning home I was still pondering the thought of being crucified, and unfortunately the thought of that was repulsive although I knew I have tasted something new, something one of a kind. Something that would change my life forever.

Well those sixteen years were anything but plain sailing. I was so used to trying to get right with God on my own steam that the good news seemed too good to be true. You see religion makes us oblivious to the heart of God. Religion obscures God for who He really is. It also makes us feel inferior when we are supposed to feel like cherished children of a loving Father.

Most of us are all too familiar with the religious notion of the enemy having to pay back seven-fold, and none of us can testify that he did anything of the sort. I mean, do you really expect satan to admit in wronging you and replacing your stuff seven-fold? But let me guess, you put it on God like we all did. Holding God accountable for something He never even promised. It's like some claiming to be immortal in the here and now, following some strange teaching and when the first person passes away, everyone who believed in this so-called immortality has their faith in God torn to shreds. That's religion right there! It has a loud mouth while the inside is a mausoleum. Religion makes you hold God accountable for things He never said. Instead of holding preachers accountable that preach that sort of nonsense, we placed it on God. When you then don't receive these things you were hoping or praying for, you start distrusting Him. And to top all of that, you hear the good news that has nothing to do with your efforts, your claiming of scriptures or a personal prophecy someone gave you early on in your christian walk, you are already so weary that you don't care about the truth anymore. Religion desensitizes us to the extent that when we actually get a glimpse of the real McCoy, it hurts, because we invested so much in this feeble, petty god we have been sustaining all along.

Unfortunately for me in that period of time and for most of the church through the ages, religion was the norm and I measured God and myself according to its gauge. In the back of my mind I knew I have tasted truth. I found myself in an identity crisis and the solution was not in acquiring the perfect identity but rather to first see what my design is. You see the symptom is an identity crisis, but the root cause of our problem is being ignorant of our design.

Long story short. I left the church and bible school and I became a plumber. About five years ago I got a call from a preacher to renovate their bathroom and of course we started talking about God. I also got a hold of some of his teaching on CD. This is my pastor and mentor today - Bertie Brits. The first teaching I listened to was: Jesus is the tithe. I found the title very intriguing. That message was exactly what I needed when I needed it. I heard the gospel as it was supposed to be preached and I found the God I was looking for up until that day. The God that is not petty concerning my shortcomings and weakness, the God that is not in dire need of my financial support. The God I was used to was nit-picky about my behavior with an audacity that I pay Him maintenance. Sounds more like a mother-in-law, employed at the revenue services, than a loving Father. You know what I mean? Just for the record: I am not against giving at all. I do have a problem with manipulation and enforcing law to get people to give though.

This book is the fruit of the ministry of Bertie Brits, sharing the love of God with a plumber. I thank God for you man!

PART 1
THE CART BEFORE THE HORSE

CHAPTER 1
A WHIFF OF SULPHUR?

To the new believer, newbie bible-school student and aspiring bible scholar, the prospect of spiritual discernment would be the ability to smell an evil spirit, on entering a room, to see a devil hovering over someone or seeing something bad in a person's eyes. Or at least that was true in my case.

Though it is still the case in some flavors of christianity to this day. If you can see a devil; You're the man! While Jesus never said anything of the sort. He would rather talk about seeing the Kingdom. Religion taught us to focus on the shortcomings of one another. To police one another, as such, to stay on the straight and narrow. But as Jesus puts it to the religious of His day. We were the blind leading the blind. Some on the other hand only want to be controversial or weird for the thrill of it, but let me tell you something, if you see Jesus in a world where everyone else sees a devil, you'll be pretty much controversial alright. Heretic would be one of your pet names. That is, if the accuser is in any way qualified to call you that in the first place. Now don't get me started on that subject!

Spiritual discernment is often confused with a critical spirit or just plain jealousy. Of which neither are spiritual. It's all an act to appear spiritual, like having a feet-washing service at your local church.

Spiritual discernment is all about seeing God and seeing the way He sees. It is crucial in our understanding of the things of God and I don't mean to intentionally redefine the meaning of words or concepts, but as soon as you see the way God sees, as soon as Jesus is your interpretation of scripture, as soon as Jesus is your point of departure in approaching theology and the embodiment of your God, you cannot but have different definitions for certain words or concepts. Will you be met with hostility in some circles? Of course! People have livelihoods, titles and reputations to defend, you know. Spiritual discernment is one of those concepts that used to get the hair on my neck to stand on end when certain *"prophets"* or *"men of God"* visited our church. In the back of my mind I would always think of it as something only a select few possessed and my natural response was to avoid them at all cost, because God would somehow show them bad things about me and they would blabber it out, for all those present to hear. I know it sounds silly, but that is how I viewed discerning the spiritual.

Fortunately my view had changed for the better and my opinion is that spiritual discernment is there for the good. To see as God sees. We have made spiritual discernment the gift of seeing a devil on the back of the old lady in church, the occasional angel on the stage as the worship band plays, the choir of devils or a massive snake on your neighbor's roof, the neighbor you cannot stand, might I add! Oh yes, and the occasional whiff of sulphur indicated the presence of an unclean spirit.

This *"gift"* of discernment was also utilized by some to determine who deserves the most honor in the room. Imagine that! Laughs! Do you see how deluded and vain religion makes us? Determining the person that deserves the most honor was made easy when Jesus said: *"The greatest among you shall be your servant."* If we are to implement Jesus' words here as a standard for appointing leadership, we'd be surprised with the outcome. Assuming this point of departure you will be as spiritual as you'll ever be.

Spiritual discernment starts when the individual sees him or herself through the Father's eyes and realize how much they are loved and treasured. How on earth is that possible? God makes it easy for us to attain seeing in the spirit per se. This happens on the basis of us acknowledging the very thing He intended from the start, when we see Him as our Father who has only good in mind for us. When we see our original design as He had planned. We get on the same page as Him so to speak. God wants to let you know that you are family. You being part of His family is supposed to be the point of departure in your christian walk and should not be presented as a reward for believing. It's as simple as that.

God is spirit and He is supposed to be all you would want to see. I am not saying you should not see various things. I'm just asking to what benefit it serves. I had been involved in countless *"deliverance sessions"* where devils were cast out of individuals and some of the counsellors would see different spirits and bindings, but failed to see how Jesus values the concerned individual, failed to see how they were a victim. I was asking then and I am still asking now how that sort of discernment helps. You know what? It doesn't. It causes an *"us and them"* mentality and it is fruitless.

As soon as you realize God's love for you and how much He values you, your inner man/spirit opens up in order for you to receive from Him. All of a sudden He makes sense and you are able to **see** the **kingdom**. See John 3. We see that Nicodemus was aware of the signs and wonders Jesus performed but He was unable to see the kingdom. **Seeing** the kingdom becomes our point of departure and then **entering** the kingdom subsequently follows when we choose to partake.

"But as it is written, Eye hath not seen, nor ear heard, neither have entered into the heart of man, the things which God hath prepared for them that love him." 1 Corinthians 2:9 KJV

At first glance the slave or legalistic mindset would identify the key to this scripture - *"them that love him."* Rightly so. But then proceed reading it as a job description, rather than seeing it for what it is. But then how else would we love God? The apostle John comes to our rescue in the following verse.

"We love him, because he first loved us." 1 John 4:19 KJV

Some translations only say: *"We love, because He first loved us."* We cannot love on our own because we have no reference to true love prior to our encounter with Jesus. The Author of love becomes our reference concerning love. So when we approach 1 Corinthians 2:9 from this perspective we no longer see love as a chore but a result of being loved by Him. This results in us seeing what He sees. We begin to see and value ourselves and others accordingly. God lets us in on

His secrets when we allow Him to love us.

In contrast with this – not realizing your value, you wouldn't be able to discern His things and He wouldn't make sense. If we are to relate to God from a religion induced inferiority complex our definitions of spiritual concepts like grace, would be a license to sin instead of divine influence unto godliness. Forgiveness would be something you have to earn and repentance would be a constant chore for personal sanctification. Being placed in Christ, would be a result of your faith. I thank God it isn't. Do you see how religion messed up the meaning of spiritual concepts beyond recognition? No wonder we need to redefine from a son in the house perspective and leave the slave mentality and interpretation behind.

A wrong angle on spiritual discernment brought on the necessity of other religious practices in order for us to deal with the things we would normally have Jesus take care of on our behalf. Practices like: Spiritual warfare, prayer warrior intercession, exorcisms, bloodline-curses, national repentance sessions, man's attempt to restore the five-fold ministry and many, many more. These practices were utilized to deal with the root but sadly the root of our problem was our point of departure. Unfortunately Jesus wasn't that point of departure.

And so the root started bearing fruit. It's like a futile attempt of constantly picking off the bad fruit from a tree, in an attempt to deem the tree good. Not going to happen. The more spiritual we got the further we drifted away from God. Let alone seeing Him, and seeing as He sees. In contrast with this spiritual concept we are used to, the more competent we are in relating to and conveying the love of God to the lost, the more relevant and spiritual we become. The person washing the feet is the important one, according to Jesus. As someone once said: *"If serving is beneath you, leadership is beyond you!"*

So how am I to discern the authenticity of a prophet or preacher presenting me with a word from the Lord? If this person is addressing you in a condescending manner and not as a child of a loving Father, treats you as the original instigator of sin, and not a victim of a system that kills – wave them good-bye and tell them I say hi and good-bye too. To put it plainly. Would that encounter be the way you would expect your loving Father to talk to you? I didn't think so either. So let it roll of your back as you make your way to the door.

You probably scanned through the table of contents and noticed that there are a lot of concepts in the chapters in part one of this book, that seem to be general knowledge to the church and the believer, but we have to cover them from a *"sons"* perspective. This is merely to broaden our understanding on these concepts so we can approach the creation story and the garden, seeing the way God sees. We change when we see ourselves the way God sees us and as a result we also see others through different eyes. All of a sudden that fat devilish snake on your neighbor's roof is nowhere to be found and all you can see is someone that our Father loves so dearly, that He gave His Son in order for that person to have His life. We start to treasure others as we ourselves are treasured by our Father. This divine love is contagious. This puts us in a perpetual thankful state.

Spiritual discernment is not about seeing devils! Never was, never will be. It is all about seeing God and His kingdom - how He operates. You then not only perceive His deeds but you also understand His ways. You understand His only motive and that is relentless love toward us. That's all there is to it! You are as spiritual as you'll ever be when you realize God's love for you. My prayer is that God shows you so much of Himself and His goodness in you and in others that you'll never see or have the need to see or smell a devil. Jesus is way more beautiful and you know what?

- He smells better too!

CHAPTER 2
GOD IS GOOD

God is good. This phrase has almost become cliché and the view of God being good with an enormous, unnerving BUT, still widely accepted in the church worldwide.

"God is good, but, he came and fetched our son, because he needed another flower in His current bouquet." Or, *"God is good, but, He sent a tornado to a certain island because of their wickedness."* Or even, *"If God is good, why did He allow so many people to be massacred in Rwanda?"*

To name only a few. I am sure you could also add some examples to the ongoing list. My response would be as follows:

First of all. We are currently living in a fallen creation. This creation is awaiting the adoption of sons, as are we.

Secondly. Man received morals and free-will, whether they are saved or not. That is part of the design of man. More on that later. Let us look at the first BUT. God does not kill anyone. Yes, I know people got killed in the old testament but hopefully by the end of this book you'll have your answer. We are all subject to this order of corruption (decay), not politicians stealing money, although that too, till Jesus comes back. I really find it hard to blame God when I know someone got drunk, got behind the steering wheel of his car, drove into a tree and was killed on impact and at the funeral the minister mentions that God picked a flower. That is not my Father's character. That is messed up. The god that does that has darkness in him and is not the Father Jesus came to reveal. The flower-picking-crap is usually my cue to get up and leave, before I disturb the peace.

Second BUT. The tornado. Have you ever read the clause in an insurance policy? *"Damages due to an act of God."* God was dealt a bad hand when it comes to natural disasters. All that comes to mind is the fact that this creation is yearning for the sons of God to be revealed. I remember Jesus quieting a storm once. If Jesus quieted a storm His Father sent then He went against the will of the Father. It can be likened to a person going against the will of God by visiting a doctor for treatment for some sickness that God supposedly inflicted on him or her. It just doesn't make sense.

Third BUT. Morals and free-will. The peacekeeping forces in Rwanda, at the time, were fully aware of the imminent threat of a genocide and still they withdrew their forces. The genocide followed as a result. So I beg of you. Please don't confuse God with stupid people, or rather in this case, corrupt people with a hidden agenda, who knew exactly what the outcome of their actions would be.

If you believe the three buts about God you are actually admitting that you believe in a being that you don't really trust yourself. I mean who would trust Him? Relationship is out the back door when distrust and uncertainty enters through the front door.

"This then is the message which we have heard of him, and declare unto you, that God is light, and in him is no darkness at all." 1 John 1:5 KJV

During the course of this book you will realize the importance of interpreting scripture with Jesus as your hermeneutic approach. Jesus is the exegesis of the Father. If your god steals, kills and destroys – allow Jesus to show you the Father.

Moral law

Speaking of morals raises some more questions. I hope this discussion will answer some of them. A synonym for morals are values. We speak about someone's morals as their values. The word *"values"*, describes it better. Let's say life is a road we all travel on. Everyone going about their day to day living. I treat/value others on this road according to the extent that I value myself. If we want the blueprint on valuing others we need to find out how much we are valued. We find this in the gospel. Am I saying unsaved people cannot have values? Not at all. What I am saying is that there is a higher form of values or morals found only in the love of God in Jesus.

Moral law was initially written down in stone in the form of the Ten Commandments to the nation of Israel. Moses was then obliged to add another six hundred and three more because of the hardness of their hearts. The law was added as a temporary supervisor to teach righteous standards and magnify sin until Christ came. The law used to be our schoolmaster until Jesus came and graduated on our behalf.

You see the law could never give us the Holy Spirit. The law could never produce a single christian.

"22 But the scripture hath concluded all under sin, that the promise by faith of Jesus Christ might be given to them that believe. 23 But before faith came, we were kept under the law, shut up unto the faith which should afterwards be revealed. 24 Wherefore the law was our schoolmaster to bring us unto Christ, that we might be justified by faith. 25 But after that faith is come, we are no longer under a schoolmaster. 26 For ye are all the children of God by faith in Christ Jesus." Galatians 3:22-26 KJV

In a sermon titled: *"Why the law cannot make us whole"* - Pastor Paul White states that the law was given to show Israel that they were no better than the nations surrounding them. And still they took pride in this ignorance. Taking pride in rule keeping is hardly something to brag about if you ask me. It actually shows that you cannot be trusted. By rule keeping you are trying to subdue another nature on the inside when in fact you were given a brand new nature in Christ.

"4 Hear, O Israel: The LORD our God is one LORD: 5 And thou shalt love the LORD thy God with all thine heart, and with all thy soul, and with all thy might." Deuteronomy 6:4-5 KJV

"18 Thou shalt not avenge, nor bear any grudge against the children of thy people, but thou shalt love thy neighbor as thyself: I am the LORD." Leviticus 19:18 KJV

Jesus quoted these two scriptures when asked which commandment is the greatest in Matthew 22.

"On these two commandments hang all the law and the prophets." Matthew 22:40 KJV

We know Jesus fulfilled both the law and the prophets -

but how? *"Love the Lord your God with all your heart...."* was fulfilled by Him loving His neighbor as Himself. Yes. We love Him because He first loved us. He came and loved us as His neighbor, His equal, and showing us our true value. God becoming man shows us our worth. *"What is man that You are mindful of us?"* We are His equal and He treats us accordingly in His Son. We now love Him and our neighbor from this standard.

"But now we are delivered from the law, that being dead wherein we were held; that we should serve in newness of spirit, and not in the oldness of the letter." Romans 7:6 KJV

"But if ye be led of the Spirit, ye are not under the law." Galatians 5:18 KJV

In ancient cultures, where reading and writing wasn't practiced, the history and culture was carried over to the next generation by recitation. Someone would recite their history under the supervision of the elders that know the history and culture very well. This then ensures the authenticity of the *"story."* Now for us the scriptures do this very thing but it lacks a very crucial component. It lacks spirit. God comes to our aid and enlighten the scriptures and especially the law when the Holy Spirit brings perspective and clarity. I don't care how bad your translation of the bible is. God's Spirit is greater than any bad translation. The most feeble of persons is potentially a mighty tool at the hand of the Holy Spirit. The Holy Spirit gives the *"story"* its original flavor and makes its power as authentic as the day it played out. He makes it real to us. Thank God for His Spirit. He is God. You can trust Him. You're in good hands.

Is it possible to obtain salvation by upholding good morals? Heavens no! And yet we have quite frequent instances where members of our society were caught in the act of adultery which resulted in "christian" businesses boycotting them. Friends, family and vague acquaintances shun or ignore them. Why is that? Let me tell you why. Within this day and age we find ourselves, people still depend on taking care of their own sin. In other words – our morals are our means of salvation. Someone that lacks that special ability to cleanse themselves, or keep themselves clean in the above mentioned case are regarded as weak and no mercy is shown. Furthermore, any sympathizer would be regarded likewise. No wonder Jesus was called all sorts of names. He was hanging out with these guys! If you can't look at those two people and see what God sees then you are part of the problem. Shunning bad behavior and praising good behavior is not a fruit of the spirit, it is only an indication that your morals are sitting in the seat meant for Jesus. Especially if you're a christian. Behavior modification cannot save you. Jesus saves you and that results in a change in your behavior. We call that the fruit of the Spirit. Him living inside you. Not you conjuring up some imaginary standard.

The law was given to show you that your morality cannot save you. Let us take a look at the instance where Jesus was called for His opinion on the woman caught in the act of adultery. Who was ready to stone her to death? The pharisees right? Right. These are the very same guys who relied on their morals to save them. You have one choice. Jesus or morality – only one can save you! Don't be a pharisee is all I say.

In conclusion. God is not, and never was the concerned little mother, writing us a to-do list on how to take on life, how to avoid the bullies and how to be the teacher's pet. He gave us His Spirit on the inside, Him living in us, to be our very life! To see our own value in Him, us valuing others accordingly, would come natural. Now that's good fruit! I mean…. morals.

The love of God

> *"Theology that starts with: "God is love, but ..."*
> *- has already missed the point." - Arthur Frymyer Jr.*

The love of God is something that is still so misunderstood in the world and in the lives of so many christians. We made the love of God something that it is not. The biggest mistake we can make is to try to love God or others, for that matter, out of our own power. We can only love God and others when we have been *"reset"* by His love. What do I mean by this? His love sets the standard. Let us take a look at Matthew 5:46-47 and see how Jesus defines man's love.

> *"46 For if ye love them which love you, what reward have ye? do not even the publicans the same? 47 And if ye salute your brethren only, what do ye more than others? do not even the publicans so?"* Matthew 5:46-47 KJV

If you practice this sort of love you are stuck in a rut of religion once again. God's love would then be dependent on your ability to love someone. Do you see that when you find yourself in religion how that limits God? His love would be limited to your feeble reach. Trust me, it is quite feeble. If change in this world depended on our ability to love others and God on our own steam, all of us would be screwed proper.

Thank God His love operates independent of, and despite our shortcomings.

14

"Herein is love, not that we loved God, but that he loved us, and sent his Son to be the propitiation for our sins."
1 John 4:10 KJV

A while back I read an article on an inmate on death row for some gruesome crimes he had committed in the United States. The reporter who was allowed into the penitentiary to interview the inmate, reported that he was the most miserable and evil person he had ever encountered. You get the picture. The inmate even said that he hates every person on earth. Imagine the warped picture this person must have had concerning family, friendship and fellowship. No person is born with this amount of hatred - I am sorry. He must have had an awful childhood and a closet filled with painful memories. His tough demeanor was just a facade to mask his wounded soul. We'll get back to our inmate friend here in a minute.

1 John 4:19 says: *"We love Him, because He first loved us."* So we only receive the capacity to love once we see God's amazing love towards us. Now, believe it or not. There is this notion in the church operating under the banner of grace that teaches that our salvation lies in loving everyone and everything right. Even celebrities, ex-pastors and talk-show hosts are up in arms about this *"new"* revelation. Sounds like new-age crap to me but let's leave it at that.

Now imagine telling our inmate friend that his salvation or in other words, him getting right with God lies in him loving everyone including God. Your gospel is that he has to apply the love that is supposedly already inside him. Let's say that's the *"good news"* you are bringing him. I sure can imagine his response. He would tell you to shove your *"good news"* where the sun don't shine, and that's putting it mildly. The reason for this response is simply because love can only be shared when it is felt first. First of all, he has no idea what love looks or feels like and secondly his salvation or plainly stated, his getting right with God, is once again dependent on his performance. An impossible task. Religion in other words.

Why would it be hard for him to comply? Simply because love at this stage of his life, does not form part of his frame of reference. His mindset just doesn't allow for love of any kind. He probably does not even love himself! When our approach is performance based religion, it would be placing this poor guy under the law, a law that is dressed up in a brand new jacket. Your christianity would leave the same bad taste in his mouth as any performance oriented religion would. No! This guy needs to hear that he has a loving Father that longs for his fellowship. A Father that sent His Son, Jesus, to bear his pain, his shortcomings, his very old man and give him His very life. A Father that holds absolutely nothing against him. I don't know about you, but that sounds like good news to me. Good news without a catch. Then, and only then would he have the ability to love. You and I and our inmate friend need to experience God's love first to get *"reset"* in the love department. This reminds me of that song by Foreigner - *"I wanna know what love is, I want you to show me."*

Repentance

2 Chronicles 7:14, South Africa's favorite verse of scripture when we need something, especially rain. Somehow a law mindset immediately thinks it wronged God and needs to make amends. Sin in this case caused God to send a drought. Usually a day of humiliation is announced. Yes, humiliation, or at least that's what the Afrikaans/English

16

dictionary says. Basically this day is announced to show God how humble and sorry we are. And we realize that our bad behavior brought this upon us - the drought that is. Growing up in the corn-capital in the Free-State I knew the drill all too well. Everyone gets dressed in their Sunday Best, goes to the "Mother church" in the centre of town and sing a couple of hymns and pray for about forty five minutes, go home and regard the rest of the day as a Sunday. I mean you wouldn't want to act like your old self too soon and jeopardize the whole day. It's hard work acting like your *"better self"* you know. This trend is yet to dissipate into the archives of the ignorance of man as it is still practiced to this day. I sometimes wish that God wouldn't send rain so people exercising this sort of religion would see that it doesn't work that way. But God always sends the rain because people like me also need it.

Being raised in a religious home, I had very little knowledge on who God really was. My great-grandma, a jolly old pentecostal lady, was God's light in my childhood. She always testified of God's goodness and His provision and with her limited knowledge of Him she still made a difference. Always a grateful heart, always ready to share the good news with someone. Now considering the fact that we were members of the Dutch Reformed Church, my mom wasn't too fond of her sharing and *"indoctrinating"* us kids with her beliefs. So when my mom wasn't around I always asked her to play us a cassette of someone's testimony. Usually these were testimonies of people that came out of the occult and accepted Jesus and I was always amazed to listen to their stories. One day we were listening to someone's testimony, a former satanist, and this particular story didn't sit well with me. Not because of the occult nature, but because of this person's encounter with the petty christian god. This person went on to say that God told him to make a list of all the sin he had ever committed and then confess the whole list. This was his means of becoming holy. So he did just that over a span of weeks. Weeks I tell you! And that was only the time spent on making the list. Aside from that, he then still had to work up the courage to confess and make amends for this list of trespasses.

All pumped up with the glorious prospect of being holy and righteous as a result of his confession, he continued to ask for forgiveness and when the list was ticked off he still felt a distance between him and God. *"God"* then told him that he killed a chicken when he was like 4 years old. In my mind that sounded a bit far fetched because I behaved much worse than that. I nearly burnt down the house when I was 4 years old. Somehow I always had it in the back of my head that God wasn't petty, but I had limited resources to prove it. My childlike reasoning was this – if you can get yourself *"clean"* with your own effort of confession and self-chastisement then you most probably didn't need Jesus. And according to my limited knowledge, you don't get to see the Father without Him, no exceptions. Thinking back on this experience I realized how God already spoke to my heart not to believe just anything I heard. You can trust the Holy Spirit. Not only for yourself, but that He would also lead others in the truth.

This notion of the testimony of the satanist with his list is still very much inherently part of the mindset of the broader church. We transition from one petty god to another by means of repentance-culture with no real change to show for it. If you think the satanist had a bad deal being deprived of God's quality of life before the repentance session, his life, following the session wouldn't be much different. Was he better off with his newly found christian god? With his new god, he still felt unwanted, unloved, underserving unless he himself, did something about it! This is exactly why repentance is the fruit of surveying substance. It is neither the key to get a sneak peak, nor a means of downpayment for substance.

Paul says: *"It's the goodness of God that causes people to repent."* not - *"your repentance makes God good!"* My goodness! We had it the other way around for far too long.

Here's why substance matters. Like with so many other terms that were misunderstood, our definition of repentance also suffered the same fate. Fear played a prominent role in getting people to repentance or to get them to convert. Our *"gospel"* was an attempt to avoid hell rather than presenting the hearer with the substance which is the new creation in Christ. This happened mainly because the gospel wasn't preached from a position of the finished work. The gospel, and I am speaking in general, was good news without substance. Do you see why your Gospel has to be good news? What do I mean by this? Our good news was some distant futuristic possibility. The hearer had to heed the message and then turn from their old life to the unknown, to uncertainty. Meanwhile the old life he possessed had substance, his own laws of right living defines him. His current life is very real to him. It had meaning, not all that good but yet it is relatable. It brought him comfort. It got him where he needed to be in his spiritual life. In a corporate view it defined his identity. Here the misinformed church comes along, demanding a turn from this way of life and in return it offers a possibility? A possibility of something better? An option without any certainty? *"What exactly do I have to turn to?"* - *"I don't want to burn! But what am I turning to?"* These are the troubling questions, to name a few, when the unbeliever is presented with a gospel of uncertainty. The saying: *"....better the devil you know than the devil you don't!"* makes perfect sense when placed in the hearer's shoes.

Let us look at it this way. We can liken this guy's current life with him owning a car. This car in spiritual terms is a rust bucket that needs constant maintenance. Certain operations of this car are only known to him. It is personalized if you like. He worked long hours to buy this and it still demands a lot of his care. This car was, and still is a huge investment and it may not look like much but he takes pride in it. This is his current religion. It *"works"* for him.

Now with this in mind. How would you recommend we go about in getting him to receive something better? For him to drive off in a better car. To give him a better deal. You see if the finished work is something foreign to you, the one that wants him to turn, you will lose him and even make it harder for someone else to reach him. Because of the fact that you imprinted a perception of God in his mind and anyone approaching him in the name of that *"god"* would be regarded without any distinction. The traditional approach to this man and his rust bucket car won't make him turn because of the simple fact that no right thinking person gives up their car as a means of getting by, for going on foot with the sudden blind faith in a distant futuristic possibility. Would you trust a total stranger with your car keys, setting out on foot to see if there's a better car for you on the other side of town? That would be expecting a bit much from a new believer don't you think? This is just me. If you approached me and told me to give up on my old car, something that I've invested so much into over the years, I would immediately look over your shoulder to see what substitute you had in store for me. Do you think I would get out of something that was my means of getting around town (life) for a promise or a possibility? Something that has yet to become a reality while my rust bucket is a tangible reality, right here, right now? I don't think so. You must be kidding! That's one of the reasons the religious church don't understand why it can't be taken seriously. Why would someone leave their current religion if all you offered was a possibility without substance? Let's say I'm that guy and I had recently replaced the tires and I'm currently saving up to have the engine serviced. I have already invested so much time and money. You then come along and try to convince me that there's a better car for me but you cannot deliver on that promise, the only thing you would leave me with, would be a bad taste in my mouth. But if you pulled up beside me with a new Rolls Royce and told me it's mine you wouldn't even have to convince me to turn away from the rust bucket car. All of my effort and money spent on the rust bucket would not even compare to the joy of receiving the Rolls Royce.

In this same way when the finished work, good news is presented, repentance needn't even be mentioned. When you present Jesus in all His glory and all He has done for the individual, it leaves little space for any further convincing. What then is the substance we need to preach? The reality right now pertaining to every human being is the risen Jesus at the right hand of God. He represents man there. Your good news should include this and not stop at the cross, hence the finished work. It's His goodness that makes us turn. Jesus as a man in the Godhead is the word of God toward man and stands as an invitation. The message this projects to mankind is the Father's view of man and that all are welcome. It is no longer a restricted area. God's high esteem of you needs no maintenance.

Confidence to approach

"14 Seeing then that we have a great high priest, that is passed into the heavens, Jesus the Son of God, let us hold fast our profession. 15 For we have not an high priest which cannot be touched with the feeling of our infirmities; but was in all points tempted like as we are, yet without sin. 16 Let us therefore come boldly unto the throne of grace, that we may obtain mercy, and find grace to help in time of need." Hebrews 4:14-16 KJV

There's a Man in the Godhead. This picture gives man confidence to approach.

Several years ago my cousin Arnold worked as a fry-cook and his wife Riana, his girlfriend back then, used to be a waitress at the same restaurant. Before they got together, he liked her but like any guy he was shy to approach her. *"What if she rejects me and I'm stuck here having to deal with her every day knowing she doesn't feel the same?"* One day while frying up steak and ribs in the kitchen the news came through the grapevine that she fancied him. He was over the moon. So like any good Lamprecht, he was working on a plan. One of his duties were to drop everyone off at their homes after work, using the restaurant's minivan. This would be the opportunity to make his move! Usually this would happen in the late evening. He went about dropping everyone whilst driving past her house about three or four times which aroused suspicion not only with her, but everyone else who knew about the rumors doing their rounds.

Finally, now with only the two of them remaining in the van, he grabbed a hold of all the courage he could get his hands on, and in a cool and composed voice proceeded: *"So, ... I hear you fancy me!"* The rest is history. A couple of years later he asked her to be his wife. This would not have been possible if they hadn't known what the other person felt. In this same way God shows us He fancies us! Paul says He reconciled the world to Himself not imputing their trespasses. This gracious act causes us to want to reconcile with Him. Reconciliation was His act of making us innocent and placing us in Christ, His Son, and regarding us likewise. The invitation into fellowship with the Godhead reads: *"There's a man in the Godhead."* This gives us confidence to approach Him. Repentance becomes turning **towards** substance (Him), instead of laboring to turn **from** something.

God is not waiting for you to become all goodie-two-shoes in your own strength. He is waiting for you to see that He has created you all goodie-two-shoes – the new man in Christ.

Now there's substance I would gladly turn to!

PART 2
THE FINISHED WORK

CHAPTER 3
UNDERSTANDING YOUR INNOCENCE

*"The lamb, unable to comprehend sin gets slaughtered
and man walks away with the lamb's conscience of sin.
The lamb's innocence." - Bertie Brits.*

I n this chapter I wish to show you that our innocence lies in the fact that we died with Christ on the cross and were raised with Him, in order for you to see God's high regard of you. Just as Adam was our role model, in the same way we now have a better role model. Jesus representing us at the right hand of the Father. The apostle Paul goes on to say that while we were dead in our sins, He raised us up with Him in Colossians 2:13. The life that was intended for man right from the start. *"So you're telling me I died and was raised without knowing it?"* Let me put it this way. Did God first consult with Adam before He created him? No? What was your question again?

Innocence restored simply means that God fixed the platform from which we believe. The platform from which we view Him and ourselves in the true light. It had to be His doing. We were unable to achieve this. This paved the way for us to get saved from the right platform. Seeing Him for who He is and seeing ourselves as He intended from even before the beginning.

In Born from Innocence, Brits shows us how the innocence of man was initiated at the baptism of Jesus by John the Baptist. *"So when did our innocence start? At the baptism of Jesus or at the cross?"* Let me explain it this way. You have always been innocent. You were not aware of this, because you were an enemy in your mind – not a real enemy. God always regarded you innocent, but our human condition limited Him to convey His true feelings toward us. So for us it became tangible at the baptism of Jesus where He took the sin of the world on Himself, and accordingly the heart of the Father was revealed to us by the way He treated mankind. He could heal the sick and forgive people without their confession or repentance, as we know it. The cross on the other hand is where the old man died. Jesus' baptism and crucifixion was God conveying the truth about our innocence. These actions were mere vehicles He used to express it in human form. So I would say both. *"But what about the people who lived between His baptism and the cross?"* Well they got a first-hand taste of how God felt about them in the form of Jesus. For them Jesus is the lamb who takes away the sin of the world in a different setting and it addresses their subjective historical context.

"Were these people born again?" No. Just as the Israelites were not made born again by the sacrifice of the lamb, likewise people are made innocent at the cross as their old man is killed. Salvation is energized by faith. Let me put it this way. You access that which is rightfully yours by

agreeing with God's view. We will see later on in the chapter why innocence is not to be confused with salvation.

We're all in the same boat

"I see dead people!" - The Apostle Paul. 2 Cor 5:14

As soon as we realize that all people, including ourselves are in the same boat, the us and them mentality disappears. All of us missed the mark in attaining godliness in our own effort and all of us were included in the crucifixion, death and resurrection of Jesus.

*"For the love of Christ constraineth us; because we thus judge, that if one died for all, **then were all dead.**"*
2 Corinthians 5:14 KJV

*"Our firm decision is to work from this focused center: One man died for everyone. That puts **everyone in the same boat.**"*
2 Corinthians 5:14 The Message

......*then all were dead.* (KJV)
......*everyone in the same boat.* (The Message)

Does *"everyone in the same boat"* mean all are saved? Not at all. It means all were forgiven or made innocent. Paul also goes on to say in verse 17 that we should no longer know anyone after the flesh. Why is that? Simply because all of us are in the same boat. All of humanity had been placed in the state of innocence. The cross accomplished this for all. The old man was crucified and that does not imply that we are automatically saved? No. Redeemed yes. Being dead and raised in Christ does not require your faith. Walking in the newness of life, being born again, requires faith. Faith is not something we should aspire for in our own effort. In the

27

presence of relationship, faith is inevitable.

The whole world was included in Jesus' death on the cross. This inclusion in Christ's death is universal and by no means universalism. It is actually hard work to confuse the two. The cross took away our old man and placed us all, all of mankind in the same boat. That boat is called innocence. I want you to think of the worst person in the history of the world. Let's take Adolph Hitler for example. I am assuming everyone is fairly familiar with his history. Now imagine yourself in the same boat as him. The very thought of that would be quite the ice-breaker at your next bible study. Don't you think?

Q: *"Are you trying to tell me that Adolph Hitler was made innocent?"*
A: Yes.
Q: *"How could that possibly be?"*
A: Romans 5:6-10 / Galatians 3:22

"6 For when we were yet without strength, in due time Christ died for the ungodly. 7 For scarcely for a righteous man will one die: yet peradventure for a good man some would even dare to die. 8 But God commendeth His love toward us, in that, while we were yet sinners, Christ died for us. 9 Much more then, being now justified by his blood, we shall be saved from wrath through him. 10 For if, when we were enemies, we were reconciled to God by the death of his Son, much more, being reconciled, we shall be saved by his life." Romans 5:6-10 KJV

"But the scripture hath concluded all under sin, that the promise by faith of Jesus Christ might be given to them that believe." Galatians 3:22 KJV

In verse 10 here we also see a distinction between *"reconciled"* and *"saved"*. The mention of reconciliation also occur in 2 Corinthians 5.

"18 And all things are of God, who hath reconciled us to himself by Jesus Christ, and hath given to us the ministry of reconciliation; 19 To wit, that God was in Christ, reconciling the world unto himself, not imputing their trespasses unto them; and hath committed unto us the word of reconciliation. 20 Now then we are ambassadors for Christ, as though God did beseech you by us: we pray you in Christ's stead, be ye reconciled to God." 2 Corinthians 5:18-20 KJV

Here we have two types of reconciliation. One is God's doing without our faith in verse 18 to 19, the other reconciliation in verse 20 has everything to do with our participation through faith.

His act of reconciliation towards us was not imputing our trespasses against us. Thus making us innocent. In other words clearing the air between us so we can see Him for who He is, seeing Jesus, our representative at His right hand, that is, seeing ourselves as we should be, then our act of reconciliation would come natural. Seeing His goodness would bring about repentance and faith.

Free to marry

Let us look at innocence from a different angle. Whenever Paul speaks of the husband and wife, he uses it as an analogy to explain the relationship between Christ and the church. How Christ cares for and cherishes the church. Ephesians 5:25.

*"2 For the woman which hath an husband is **bound by the law to her husband** so long as he liveth; but **if the husband be dead**, she is loosed from the law of her husband. 3 So then if, while her husband liveth, she be married to another man, she*

shall be called an adulteress: but if her husband be dead, she is free from that law; so that she is no adulteress, though she be married to another man. 4 Wherefore, my brethren, ye also are become dead to the law by the body of Christ; that ye should be married to another, even to him who is raised from the dead, that we should bring forth fruit unto God. 5 For when we were in the flesh, the motions of sins, which were by the law, did work in our members to bring forth fruit unto death. 6 But now we are delivered from the law, that being dead wherein we were held; that we should serve in newness of spirit, and not in the oldness of the letter." Romans 7:2-6 KJV

*"2 For instance, a wife is legally tied to her husband while he lives, but if he dies, she's free. 3 If she lives with another man while her husband is living, she's obviously an adulteress. But if he dies, she is quite **free to marry** another man in good conscience, with no one's disapproval. 4 So, my friends, this is something like what has taken place with you. When Christ died he took that entire rule-dominated way of life down with him and left it in the tomb, leaving you **free to marry a resurrection life** and **bear offspring of faith** for God. 5 For as long as we lived that old way of life, doing whatever we felt we could get away with, sin was calling most of the shots as the old law code hemmed us in. And this made us all the more rebellious. In the end, all we had to show for it was miscarriages and stillbirths. 6 But now that **we're no longer shackled** to that domineering mate of sin, and out from under all those oppressive regulations and fine print, we're **free** to live a new life in the freedom of God."*
Romans 7:2-6 The Message

Paul uses marriage as an analogy to describe us (the woman) bound to the law (the husband). To put it plainly. The wife is bound to the husband as long as he lives. We didn't know of any better. This marriage is called religion. Us submitting to a standard by which we measure God, others and ourselves. After the likeness of the first Adam we did this willingly but there was no other alternative. No other, better husband. All of mankind were bound to this husband. We were intimate and had children together. Children that brought us even more shame. We were going nowhere slowly. All of us have seen the classic wedding scene in the movies when the minister asks the congregation whether anyone has any legal objection to the joining of so and so in the sacrament of holy matrimony. Fortunately this does not mean your future mother-in-law has the power to stop you from marrying her daughter. This is a legality that has to be performed to establish whether any of the two people concerned are not already married and thus still bound to that prior commitment by law. In this same way Jesus came onto the scene under the law and *"took care"* of the law husband in an *"Al Pacino"* sort of way. You know as in the movie - *"The Godfather."* The quote, "until *death do us part"* in our wedding vows was probably derived from this next verse:

*" For the woman which hath an husband is **bound by the law to her husband** so long as he liveth; but **if the husband be dead,** she is loosed from the law of her husband."*
Romans 7:2 KJV

By *"taking care"* of the law husband the little *"sin"* children's supply was cut off simultaneously. The law husband could never produce Godly fruit in us. Now we were single again. In making us innocent Jesus dealt with the belief system that brought forth death in Adam, in whose image we procreated, hence rendering mankind **free to marry** as the Message translation refers to it.

Free to marry does not mean that you are automatically married to the new Husband. It means you are free to marry or single. The state the first Adam possessed before the fall. This free-to-marry state is what we call innocence or in-Christ. This free to marry state is not our salvation. It is the removal of guilt and condemnation from us. Everything that was contrary to our original design that was nailed to the cross of Jesus. We will discuss the dynamics of marriage later on, in the design of man.

Now that we have established that the death of the old (law) husband does not automatically make us married to the new Husband, but it only served as an act to legally end the marriage, we need to find out how we then get married to this new Husband.

"For whosoever shall call upon the name of the Lord shall be saved." Romans 10:13 KJV

The word *"name"* in this verse is translated as follows:
Name
G3686 Strong's

ὄνομα
onoma

on'-om-ah
From a presumed derivative of the base of G1097(compare G3685); a *"name"* (literally or figuratively), (*authority*, *character*): - called, (+ sur-) name (-d).

Now Romans 10:13 reads as follows:

*"For whosoever shall call on the **authority** or **character** of the Lord shall be saved."*

This would also mean that the individual confessing this, subjects him or herself to God's authority and character. He would then also agree with God's view concerning him/her. Acknowledging God's authority is true humility.

*"For whosoever shall call on the **surname** or
to be **surnamed by** the Lord shall be saved."*

This here, is the way the Gospel works. He stepped into our dark world and ended our marriage with the law husband. That was something we could not do by ourselves because we simply did not have that in ourselves or even in our frame of reference. Then He proposes to us. Not imputing our trespasses to us, He shows us that the table is cleared and our slate is clean. He shows us His goodness. That very same goodness causes us to want to get to know Him. He courts us like a real gentleman. I can't see how christians can possibly view innocence and inclusion as God forcing Himself on us. It is His goodness that draws me. I speak for myself.

Here it is again in brief. You were married to the law husband. Jesus took care of the law husband legally. You became single. Free to marry – Romans 7:3
You survey His goodness and choose to put His surname behind your name - Romans 10:13.

Putting someone's surname behind your name in our day means your'e married, no longer single. In biblical terms it means you're betrothed. Almost like married, but our marriage to the Lamb will be consummated when He gives us immortality. So yes we are married to Him and one with Him. When He returns -
"we shall be like Him (immortal)" - Paul.

You are saved by agreeing with the opinion He already has of you. You now enjoy His quality of life that is born from that belief-system. How easy was that?

*"19 To wit, that God was in Christ, **reconciling** the world unto himself, **not imputing their trespasses** unto them; and hath committed unto us the word of reconciliation. 20 Now then we are ambassadors for Christ, as though God did beseech you by*

*us: we pray you in Christ's stead, **be ye reconciled** to God."*
2 Corinthians 5:19-20 KJV

In the above verse we also see that God is committed to reconciliation by not judging us according to our petty human standards. He sees us without sin. He sees us as He sees His own Son.

*" To wit, that God was in Christ, **reconciling** the world unto himself, not imputing their trespasses unto them; and hath committed unto us the word of reconciliation."*
2 Corinthians 5:19 KJV

Reconciling
G2644 Strong's

καταλλάσσω
katallassō
kat-al-las'-so

F r o m G2596 a n d G236; **t o** *change* **mutually**, that is, (figuratively) **to** *compound* **a difference**: - reconcile.

to change mutually *- a mutual exchange*

God knows exactly how to approach us. He knows we are enemies in our minds, believing the wrong thing about Him. He knows we have a religion induced inferiority complex. How many times does the bible record an angel of the Lord having to reassure the hearers not to fear? Anything that looked like it could be God would be a reason for running or shying away. God was feared with the wrong sort of fear. So when He makes Himself known, we find it hard to reconcile the god we harbored in our minds with the one on display in the life of Jesus. Yet this is not the reconciliation I wish to discuss. How would God go about informing you of your value – the fact that He regards you as His equal?

Let us look at the two parties involved in the exchange. God and man. The currency rendered equals the value of the goods bought. What does this mean? God paid with His own Son to buy you back legally. He took your sin on Himself and that sin took Him to the cross. You are of high value to Him. He gave Himself.

Mutual exchange is also known as home swap nowadays. This is where tenants of two different places of dwelling decide to swop out homes. In this act of reconciliation God says: *"I am more than willing to settle for you if you are willing to settle for me."* Do you see the humility of this great God?

Now the idea of home swap sounds great, but what if there's a difference in value? What if one of these properties are a bit more upmarket than the other? This is where the second meaning of reconciling comes to our aid. To compound a difference.

God wants to inform you of His high regard of you. This is not to be confused with your salvation. This is the platform from which you believe. This innocence is the only platform on which He wants to build relationship. Imagine telling your spouse prior to getting married that somewhere along the line in your relationship they would have the bright prospect of being your equal. Good luck with that! I can only imagine my wife's facial expression on sharing that revelation with her! Laughs! You know what, you would still be single and I'm not sure if the other person would want anything to do with you. God knew He couldn't approach us by being condescending and expecting us to acknowledge His superiority in some weird religious way. I am by no means making lightly of His superiority. He is in fact the only one that could save us from the wrong belief system that killed us and ultimately, the body of death. That is why the lamb is worthy.

God regards you His equal to the extent that His view towards you is displayed in Him not taking your trespasses into consideration. God cannot influence you to possess what He possesses unless you are convinced that He regards you as His equal.

to compound a difference/
making up *the difference*

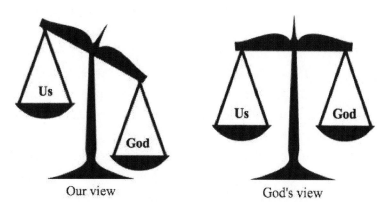

Our view   God's view

Fig 1.   Fig 2.

Consider the scales of figure 1. and figure 2. The first scale is our view of us and God. The second is God's view. In order for us to see ourselves the way He sees us, He made up the difference. God, knowing full well we had a view that our trespasses were a hindrance between us and Him, took it out of the way. The very wedge in our minds, we thought was a hindrance was taken out of the way, showing us that He doesn't judge us by that. He **makes up the difference** we thought existed between us and Him. Sin was never a problem for Him. Only in Jesus could He show us just that. In 2 Corinthians 5:20, Paul goes on to say that we should be reconciled to God. Does this mean we need to compound or make up the difference in our own effort? No. Our act of reconciliation is simply relying on His act of reconciliation. It is agreeing with what He had already done. He made up the difference. Our Father knows we suffer from inferiority complex which was brought on by the illusion of separation and He knows exactly how to approach our mindset. The separation that we thought existed between us makes us think we don't weigh up to His expectations. This is where He then compounds or *"makes up"* the difference. He tipped the scales in our favor. The slate is clean. The tables are cleared. His act makes us want to reconcile with Him. This equal scale state of innocence is the point of departure in our walk with God and it is not a reward of our effort or faith. Faith follows this state. Faith comes by hearing the Word of God concerning you!

The second scale had been His view concerning YOU all along. God's connect toward us is displaying His view of us in the incarnation of Jesus. Our connect with Him is to agree with His view concerning us! His word concerning you is not smeared with your wrongdoing! It bares the stamp of His approval. Your list of shortcomings and not *"making"* it was nailed to His cross. It was done away with. It stayed behind in the grave. It did not get up when Jesus was raised. God's view or opinion of His Son was raised up. He has this same view concerning you!

Reconciliation between two parties is helped along with the instigated act of showing the other party that there is no difference between the two of them. Showing the other party that they are not inferior to you. That you are in fact equals. Let us take a husband and wife whose marriage is on the rocks. Would it be wise to try to reconcile with the other person by pointing out their weaknesses or would it be better to say:

"Listen husband/wife, I know we've both said and done things we're not proud of and I am willing to put that behind us and give this another shot. My view of you is not what you think it is. I am not holding anything against you!"

Do you suppose this person would get results? I know he/she would. This is the very same approach God has towards us. He knew we were enemies in our minds to the extent that we thought bad stuff about Him and about ourselves. He knew exactly how to remedy that. He came and romanced us on our level. He is madly in love with YOU!

The following is a grace oriented take on reconciliation by Lee O'Hare. Lee is the founder of the Facebook group called: *Posse of Online Spiritual Misfits*, and he is set out to serve the body of Christ.

"To wit, that God was in Christ, reconciling the world unto himself, not imputing their trespasses unto them; and hath committed unto us the word of reconciliation."
2 Corinthians 5:19 KJV

"It is so important to recognize that it says God was reconciling the world to Himself, NOT that He was reconciling Himself to the world. There is a big difference between the two. Nowhere in the New Testament will you read anything about God reconciling Himself to us, because He never needed to be reconciled because He was never

against us! It was WE that needed to be reconciled to Him because we had become alienated against him in our minds, as it says in Colossians 1:21. The enmity was and always has been one-sided and it was all in our minds - it was an illusion. It was us that were against God because of our foolish and darkened thinking. He has never been against us. He was never our enemy. He has always been seeking us with restorative love and compassion desiring only to reconcile us to Himself and heal and restore the relationship that had been torn. THAT is what was happening at the cross."
- Lee O'Hare.

Fulfilling the law

Jesus did not come to teach us to be faithful and submitting to the law husband. But how did He take care of the law husband? So many times when sharing the gospel and how Jesus came to fulfill the law, you get interrupted by the odd person who defends the law by claiming the following: *"Jesus didn't come to destroy the law but to fulfill it."* They mention this with an audacity as if to say that they themselves are also able to fulfill the law. First of all. He was the only one who could fulfill the law. It was addressed to Him.

"Then said I, Lo, I come: in the volume of the book it is written of me." Psalm 40:7 KJV

"And beginning at Moses and all the prophets, he expounded unto them in all the scriptures the things concerning himself." Luke 24:27 KJV

Fulfilling the law should be seen in the same manner we see Jesus fulfilling prophecy. Let's use Matthew 8:17 as an example.

*"That it might be **fulfilled** which was spoken by Esaias the **prophet**, saying, Himself took our infirmities, and bare our sicknesses."* Matthew 8:17 KJV

Only Jesus could fulfill the prophecies concerning Him. This was also the case with the law. It was addressed to Him and something only He could fulfill. Now let us look at the meaning of the word fulfill.

Fulfill
G4137 Strong's

: to make replete, i.e. (literally) **to cram** (a net), **level up** (a hollow), or (figuratively) to **furnish** (or imbue, diffuse, influence), **satisfy**, execute (an office), **finish** (a period or task), verify.

To cram in a net. To level up a hollow. Pretty much sounds like our equivalent in today's language of filling a glass to the brim with water. There is no space for any more water. So if Jesus fulfilled the law, what can you possibly add to that from a perspective of human effort. Are you kidding me? This reminds me of a hymn we used to sing in church. Here's my direct translation from the Afrikaans. *"Should I go empty handed, should I meet my Lord this way."* Looking back at this hymn I am thinking: What on earth could you possibly have to offer you silly person?

The law was prescribed to Jesus to fulfill. Not man. God gave it as a prescription to Him to fulfill something man could not do. A standard man could not live up to. God became a man to keep and fulfill the law as a human and in doing so he removed the law.

"Do we then make void the law through faith? God forbid: yea, we establish the law." Romans 3:31 KJV

Establish the law? What is Paul on about? Is Paul trying to tell us to keep the law? No not at all. This is the same as the meaning of Romans 8:1. What Paul is trying to convey here is that when we relate to the law in spirit we are actually upholding, establishing it for what it really is. We relate to it as a standard Jesus achieved on our behalf. On the other hand the flesh is inclined to try and keep the law.

"Wherefore the law is holy, and the commandment holy, and just, and good." Romans 7:12 KJV

Holy means set apart. It belongs to someone else. It's like a prophecy that is lying in wait for the person concerned to fulfill it. This person is Jesus. The law was His to fulfill. Our job is not to try to fulfill the law but to believe on Jesus who fulfilled it on our behalf. The law was never yours to fulfill!

Understanding forgiveness

Forgiveness has the same tinge to it as the *"free to marry"* state we see in Romans 7:2-6. In both these instances we see the law husband on the one hand and us, the woman, on the other being sent away. Leaving us, the woman free. Free to choose.

Forgive
G863 Thayer's

ἀφίημι
aphiēmi

- to send away
- to bid going away or depart
- of a husband divorcing his wife

Forgiveness in the new testament is pretty much a done deal and referred to as past tense. Something that had already happened. You, the woman was sent away. Away from that marriage. You are no longer legally bound to the law husband. Considering the above we can safely say that forgiveness is a legal divorce between us and the law. Forgiveness can never be our doing because we could not free ourselves from the law. Someone else, someone our kind had to do it on our behalf, and do it legally. That is why the incarnation of God in human flesh, under the law of Moses was necessary to bring this about.

Forgiveness in the old testament on the other hand was a whole different ball-game. It was all wrapped up in conditions and requirements which needed our compliance to make it work. Paul and the early preachers of the gospel did not preach conditional forgiveness or as a requirement but rather announced it to the hearer as something that was already theirs.

"Be it known unto you therefore, men and brethren, that through this man is preached unto you the forgiveness of sins."
Acts 13:38 KJV

New testament forgiveness, or the actual preaching of the gospel does not require our confession or repentance, it rather causes repentance. Your sin is not sent away the day you confess it. It was sent away with the Lamb that took it on Himself.

"The next day John seeth Jesus coming unto him, and saith, Behold the Lamb of God, which taketh away the sin of the world." John 1:29 KJV

Yes, but what about 1 John 1:9?

"If we confess our sins, he is faithful and just to forgive us our sins, and to cleanse us from all unrighteousness."
1 John 1:9 KJV

Considering the context, the answer is quite simple. This particular piece of scripture is not applicable to everyone. John was addressing the gnostics of the day. The preceding and proceeding verses illuminates the context of what the apostle John was trying to convey to his readers. Clearly these were people claiming to be righteous outside of what God has done for them in Christ. Verse eight and verse ten is clear on that. How many times have you testified about your faith to someone and their response was something along the lines of: *"You know, I worship God in my own way."* Though this might sound sincere, this was also the mentality the apostle John had to deal with in 1 John 1:9. The context of this scripture is not that we gain forgiveness as a result of our confession, but rather that the righteousness of God cannot be found outside of Christ.

Jesus' forgiveness was unconditional. He announced it to many during His ministry. When did the church's forgiveness become conditional? We are to announce forgiveness rather than require it. His forgiveness resets mankind to their original design. The platform to be receptive of His life. He has to make way, clear out the cupboards so to speak so there is space to contain the life He wants to give you. Out with the old. In with the new. This new testament forgiveness then goes hand in hand with innocence. Returning to God's original intent. For you to obtain His life.

Your are forgiven/divorced from your old belief system to the extent that God's judgement of you is as if you were never involved with wrong belief. Your innocence is as if you are a newly created being, ready for a relationship with your

Father. This is what Jesus has done for you fully identifying with you, as you. This clean slate, innocence mood was prevalent in the garden.

You died with Him

"When He was crucified all of us were crucified there with Him. Must we ask God to crucify us? Never! When Christ was crucified we were crucified; and His crucifixion is past therefore ours cannot be future. That we have died in Christ is not merely a doctrinal position, it is an eternal and indisputable fact."
- *Watchman Nee*

"For ye are dead, and your life is hid with Christ in God."
Colossians 3:3 KJV

All of us have probably heard at least one sermon on dying to ourselves. Unfortunately this notion has no scriptural basis as there is not a single scripture in the whole of the bible that tells the believer to die to him or herself. I actually went and looked for some and found three that sound vaguely similar to the topic. The problem is that in the right context they have no connection with the believer having to die to self.

First verse:
He must increase, but I must decrease...

"29 He that hath the bride is the bridegroom: but the friend of the bridegroom, which standeth and heareth him, rejoiceth greatly because of the bridegroom's voice: this my joy therefore is fulfilled. 30 He must increase, but I must decrease."
John 3:29-30 KJV

Here John the baptist explains the role of the old testament prophets that prophesied concerning the Messiah. He refers to himself and the prophetic as the friend of the Bridegroom.

Followed by: *"He must increase, but I must decrease"* - meaning the prophetic should fade out and allow the One who was prophesied about to enjoy prominence in the spotlight. We see the same scenario play out at the mount of transfiguration when Jesus went up the mountain and Moses and Elijah appeared. Peter was astonished at this and immediately thought it would be a nice place to stay. I mean what better place to build something for the three coolest guys in history, all in one place? It would be like a landmark for all to see. If this occurred in our day we would probably suggested they each do a handprint in cement on a sidewalk in Hollywood. But then God interrupted Peter and said:

"....This is my beloved Son, in whom I am well pleased; hear ye him." Matthew 17:5b KJV

Thus putting things in perspective - that is, having Jesus enjoy prominence above the prophetic. Jesus should be heard out, so to speak. And thus the phrase: *"He must increase, but I must decrease"* has no connection as pertaining to the believer having to die to self. The context of the scripture simply does not allow that.

Second verse:
I die daily...

"I protest by your rejoicing which I have in Christ Jesus our Lord, I die daily." 1 Corinthians 15:31 KJV

At first glance it sure looks like Paul is dying to himself on a daily basis. If this was true then we are actually saying that the cross did not take away our sin and God has to look at us through glasses smeared with the blood of Jesus. That is just a slave interpretation of scripture, as we are aware that Jesus is already God's opinion about us.

This verse is also one of those where we see the true context when we read the proceeding or the preceding verse. In this case we see the preceding verse, come to our aid.

"And why stand we in jeopardy every hour?"
1 Corinthians 15:30 KJV

When Paul says: *"I die daily"* he is expressing the fact that he is at risk of getting killed for preaching the gospel on a daily basis. I assume most of you reading this are not in this perilous situation from day to day. Thus *"I die daily"* does not pertain to the believer having to die to self. The fact is that you are already dead.

Third verse:

Take up your cross and follow me...

"23 But he turned, and said unto Peter, Get thee behind me, Satan: thou art an offence unto me: for thou savourest not the things that be of God, but those that be of men. 24 Then said Jesus unto his disciples, If any man will come after me, let him deny himself, and take up his cross, and follow me. 25 For whosoever will save his life shall lose it: and whosoever will lose his life for my sake shall find it." Matthew 16:23-25 KJV

To properly grasp this we'll first have to look at the preceding two verses to understand the context and the setting of verse 24.

"21 From that time forth began Jesus to shew unto his disciples, how that he must go unto Jerusalem, and suffer many things of the elders and chief priests and scribes, and be killed, and be raised again the third day. 22 Then Peter took him, and began to rebuke him, saying, Be it far from thee, Lord: this shall not be unto thee." Matthew 16:21-22 KJV

Here we have Jesus telling His disciples what He would

endure and then ultimately suffer death at the hand of the jews and He also mentioned His resurrection. He knew what sort of death He would suffer. Crucifixion was the means used by the romans to execute criminals. He was addressing their concept of penalty of the day. The cross in their day meant certain death, preceded by agonizing suffering. Now imagine Peter taking Jesus out of hearing distance of the other disciples and cussing Him out for not restoring Israel the way he imagined it. Such nerve!

Peter still had a carnal mind and Jesus corrected him and others that had the same mind that following Him meant you should get accustomed to the fact that you would be rejected, shunned and even killed. Taking up your cross did not mean dying to yourself then and it sure doesn't mean dying to yourself now. Nothing changed. The measure of persecution over the world for following Jesus, and preaching the gospel varies from place to place and we should know that not all would take kindly to it. Taking up your cross in Jesus' day simply meant that you would probably be met with hostility for following Him. Jesus and His disciples were in direct opposition to the religion at the order of the day. A pretty different scene from most of us christians today. So no. Taking up your cross has nothing to do with you dying to yourself.

"What about denying yourself in verse 24?" Let me put it this way. If you made your peace with the fact that you could die following Jesus, you pretty much denied yourself in my books. Denying yourself in that sense has little to do with dying to yourself, or ridding yourself of the old man.

You died with Him. Your old man is dead. Imagine having to go to war to defeat an enemy and you have to kill him in order for you to have victory. In our case we would supposedly need to kill our old man in order to have victory in our christian walk. On your way one of your spies meets you on his return from the battleground, out of breath and overwhelmed with joy he shares the joyous news that the enemy is dead, kaput! You realize that you won without having to lift a finger. Instantaneous victory. Let us place ourselves in the criteria of the following analogy used by Paul in Romans 10:15

"How beautiful upon the mountains are the feet of him that bringeth good tidings, that publisheth peace; that bringeth good tidings of good, that publisheth salvation; that saith unto Zion, Thy God reigneth!" Isaiah 52:7 KJV

First of all. When a messenger makes the effort to bring good news of victory from the battlefield, it had better be good news. Good news is not - *"Hey you guys! Great news. We stand a chance of winning!"* No. Great news is - *"WE WON!"* I want to tell you that God was good before you even knew about Him. He has taken action against that which kills us before we could give Him our consent. That is why it is important to grab a hold of the gospel of grace. Now believe it or not, this behavior modification gospel is what some in the church would call good news. The real good news on the other hand is that the enemy was already dead and we were handed the victory. We won! Why does Isaiah accentuate the feet of the messenger? Well do you think the type of news would affect the messenger? I guess his demeanor and the way he ran spelled out exactly what he was about to tell those awaiting his news. Let alone his face! I remember when we did outreaches and missions and we weren't too excited about it. I mean, religion made me miserable and I thought, well if it made me so miserable I should probably not tell anyone or else they'll also end up miserable and blame me for it. If your gospel is not energizing you with a zest for His life and sharing His life with others then you should probably keep it to yourself. Sharing that would just make more work for someone else coming after you, in an effort to share the real good news.

Secondly, when the messenger announces the *"good news"* it indicates that the enemy is defeated. Past tense. Not some future possibility. It can never be future because then he would have lied. Our victory is past tense and the old man is already dealt with. Now this is exactly what Jesus has done for you. He killed off the old man. The old man you were struggling with. You were included in His death. Paul says I am crucified with Christ. When you and I realize this great truth that we are already dead we won't struggle so much with ourselves, I mean how do you struggle with a dead person? Am I saying everyone is experiencing the fullness of God? No, innocence is only the start and a mighty fine place to kick off your christian walk.

We all have a struggle with ourselves on the inside at some stage of our lives. This is usually a time before we come to know the Lord. Some of us aren't that fortunate and sit in church with this continuous struggle raging inside of us. This is our old man that constantly needs to be subdued with all sorts of *"christian"* behavior modification. He demands scripture quotations to keep him at bay. *"I am the righteousness of God in Christ!"*- was my favorite , though I remained clueless to what it meant. Does that look like the victorious christian life? Are you kidding me? The church has become an international AA meeting where we get up and confess we are sinners and we've been dry for so-and-so long. A defeated existence. Another day, another battle. But when we see we are included in His death and our old man is dead. It is like a light that has been turned on in a dark room. You can't fight a dead person. Imagine the relief. This is good news! This was intended by God to be the starting line of man's walk with Him. Most of us got scared into the faith and after recuperating we find that God isn't that bad, actually not bad at all. I wish I had heard this earlier. Maybe I would have had less gray hair.

We were the veil

Relationship can only function from innocence/right standing. I can only approach you with confidence if I am convinced that you are not holding anything against me. In Hebrews 10:19-20 we see innocence, us being included in Jesus' death and how that obtained us entry into God's very presence.

"19 Having therefore, brethren, boldness to enter into the holiest by the blood of Jesus, 20 By a new and living way, which he hath consecrated for us, through the veil, that is to say, his flesh;" Hebrews 10:19-20 KJV

Most people are not aware that mankind was part of the tabernacle and later the temple in the old testament. At first glance one might think it would be preposterous to even harbor such a way of thinking but if we study the scriptures we see how all this falls into place and makes perfect sense. The reader would probably object to such a notion with the following response. *"Man was way to sinful and dirty to make out any part of the temple. You must be mistaken."* I know that would have been my response too a while back. Hang in there and allow me to explain. Let us take a look at the commission to build the tabernacle. God commanded

Moses to build the tabernacle exactly as he showed Him and the veil was a crucial part of God's design. The veil represented flesh. You see the key here lies in the last two words of this piece of scripture. *"His flesh."* If we take the next verse into account.

"For the love of Christ constraineth us; because we thus judge, that if one died for all, then were all dead:"
2 Corinthians 5:14 KJV

We then see that we were part of His flesh. Now go back to Hebrews 10:20. His flesh is likened to the veil of the temple. Our flesh is His flesh! When Jesus said: *"It is finished!"* and gave up the ghost that very same veil tore in half. Meaning our old man was killed. Taken out of the way. The key to the christian's victory in life starts here. Victory has absolutely nothing to do with you dealing with sin or overcoming sin. It has to do with you having a revelation that the person you are struggling with (yourself) was already killed off at the cross. The veil signifies us standing in our own way in getting to God as we were enemies of God in our minds, not real enemies. Remember it was man's choice to have the Mosaic covenant and that covenant required a veil between man and God.

With the veil now open - does that mean everyone is saved? No. Redeemed? Yes. It means you can now enter in with boldness, with a clear conscience. The bread and the wine of the new covenant announces the end of this old way of relating to God and declares it obsolete. Have you tried to ask someone a favor when you know they clearly can't stand the sight of you. Now this same mentality is prevalent in the mind of man in his relating to God. God should be mad and upset at me or I am inadequate or inferior. These are all temperaments and attributes we ascribe to God when it's clearly not true. John 3:16 does not read: *"For God was so mad that He sent ...."* It rather reads: *"God so loved the world!"* If that's in place – you're on the right track. Mankind was caught up in a inferiority complex and felt obliged to give his best in trying to restore relations with God or at least keep the unknown imaginary fury of God at bay. Praise God for revealing His love towards us in Jesus!

I am aware that this chapter is quite the mouthful. But it is important that the reader understands the concept of innocence and that the right foundation is laid in understanding the happenings in the garden. Innocence is the state in which the first Adam was created. Adam fell from this state. He did not fall from a salvation state. Popular religion states that Adam had it all and some even go as far as saying that he flew around in outer space and all. We have no evidence that any of these claims are true. Adam, or rather the woman was to acknowledge her design and in doing that acquire God's intended identity. In other words Adam did not receive Jesus, yet Jesus was at His disposal. Man remained a living soul and the *"hole"* Jesus was supposed to fill was occupied by a identity contrary to the original intent of the Father.

You were raised with Him

*"14 For the love of Christ constraineth us; because we thus judge, that if one died for all, then were all dead: 15 And that he died for all, that they which live should not henceforth live unto themselves, but unto him which **died for them, and rose again**."*
2 Corinthians 5:14-15 KJV

*"5 Even when we were dead in sins, hath quickened us together with Christ, (by grace ye are saved;) 6 And hath **raised***

us up together, and made us sit together in heavenly places in Christ Jesus: 7 That in the ages to come he might shew the exceeding riches of his grace in his kindness toward us through Christ Jesus." Ephesians 2:5-7 KJV

"*11 In whom also ye are circumcised with the circumcision made without hands, in putting off the body of the sins of the flesh by the circumcision of Christ: 12 Buried with him in baptism, wherein also ye are risen with him through the faith of the operation of God, who hath raised him from the dead. 13 And you, being dead in your sins and the uncircumcision of your flesh, hath he quickened together with him, having forgiven you all trespasses;*" Colossians 2:11-13 KJV

If dying with Him wasn't enough, He also took the liberty to raise you with Him. What a mind boggling thought! Being raised alongside Jesus signifies the born again experience and implies God's view and opinion of man. What exactly is His opinion about man? God placing mankind in Christ and then placing Jesus in the Trinity, shows His high esteem concerning man. His high regard for man. Jesus in human form in the God-head right at this very moment is the word of God concerning you! Has His opinion changed all of a sudden? No. He could only express His feelings towards us in the incarnation of Himself in human flesh, aiding us to better relate to Him.

"*55 But he, being full of the Holy Ghost, looked up stedfastly into heaven, and saw the glory of God, and Jesus standing on the right hand of God, 56 And said, Behold, I see the heavens opened, and the Son of man standing on the right hand of God.*" Acts 7:55-56 KJV

Stephen saw Jesus at the right hand of God in verse 55. He could have said I see Jesus, but He interpreted the vision as the Son of man standing at the right hand of God. Son of man meaning He is representing mankind. Jesus in human form in the Trinity is like a giant billboard showing God's high esteem of mankind. Showing off man's original design.

In conclusion all of these phrases in scripture ....in the same boat ....died with Him ....free to marry ....if one died for all, then all died, clearly spell INNOCENCE!

Now to clarify some misconceptions surrounding innocence. Innocence is not to be confused with salvation (subjective participation). God does not need your consent to make you innocent. Your innocence does not depend on your free-will. Being made innocent or being included does not mean you are enjoying His quality of life. It would be like showing me your letter of good standing with the revenue services and then expecting me to assume you are automatically on their board of directors. Good luck with that! Forgiveness provides a platform of innocence from which we see our original design. A platform from which we see ourselves and God in the right light. I like to call this platform a clean slate from which you can choose your source of life, free from obligation and guilt. You will never see your original design from a law perspective. You will never see your original design from a place where you have a works mentality. Because your innocence has absolutely nothing to do with your works or ability.

Drawing all _ _ _ to Him?

"And I, if I be lifted up from the earth, will draw all (men) unto me." John 12:32 KJV

In studying this verse we find that the word *"men"* was omitted in the original greek. Scholars and bible translators have placed *"men"* in that gap with good reason and yet some disagree on this.

Here's why *"men"* or mankind perfectly fits. When we read John 12:34 we see in what capacity Jesus is speaking. He refers to Himself as the Son of man. This also forms the context by which we can interpret verse 32.

*"The people answered him, We have heard out of the law that Christ abideth for ever: and how sayest thou, The **Son of man** must be lifted up? who is this Son of man?"*
John 12:34 KJV

The context here is *"Son of man."* What would, for instance, the son of donkey draw to himself? Wanna take a wild guess? ....donkeys? That's right! That is why the Son of Man draws all MEN (mankind) unto Himself! ALL of them!

"And the Lord said unto Moses, Make thee a fiery serpent, and set it upon a pole: and it shall come to pass, that every one that is bitten, when he looketh upon it, shall live."
Numbers 21:8 KJV

"14 And as Moses lifted up the serpent in the wilderness, even so must the Son of man be lifted up: 15 That whosoever believeth in him should not perish, but have eternal life. 16 For God so loved the world, that he gave his only begotten Son, that whosoever believeth in him should not perish, but have everlasting life. 17 For God sent not his Son into the world to condemn the world; but that the world through him might be saved. 18 He that believeth on him is not condemned: but he that believeth not is condemned already, because he hath not believed in the name of the only begotten Son of God."
John 3:14-18 KJV

This verse is an excellent example of inclusion in order for us not to confuse it with other concepts. In John 3:14, Jesus refs back to Numbers 21:8. On studying this we see the serpent was lifted up and all those that were bitten by the serpents were "included" in the serpent on the pole. Being included without their consent and without their knowledge wasn't their salvation and still isn't for us today. **Them that looked** upon the serpent in Numbers 21:8 and us that **believe on Jesus** are saved. In this exercise God is inviting us to see as He sees. You see, he wants you to see for yourself that the person you thought you were to Him (your old man) is dead. To Him that person never existed, but He has to take us through the paces, taking the long way, to show us just that. When we get that, we get a glimpse of His great love and our inclusion into it.

Inclusion is the finished work and salvation is obtained by believing the finished work. By including us in Him, Jesus redeemed our original design. He had to assume our form to be able to redeem it. Thus faith in this finished work (being included) results in salvation.

Adam and innocence

Adam's participation wasn't needed in order for God to create him innocent. Neither was ours. To understand Adam's innocence better we need to look at the in-Christ reality. The first Adam fell from God's design. Last Adam included all that were in the first, in order for us to see that when the Last Adam died, our old nature went extinct. The Last Adam was the very last specimen of our old human race. He had all our baggage on Him since His baptism all the way to the cross where it killed Him - *"The wages of sin is death."* When He died, we all died, when He was buried, we were buried, when He was raised, we were raised. He became the firstborn from the dead. He was the very last of the old man and He became the very first of the new man. A new mankind. When He ascended we ascended with Him to the father's right hand. So when we put our faith in Jesus we are actually believing that He actually included us in Him, in His finished work, as He conquered death and sin in our human form and when all was done, He assumed His (our rightful) place, right next to the Father.

The thing that distinguishes inclusion (image/design-restored/innocence) from universalism is identity. Identity has to be acquired by the individual in order for him/her to enjoy the fullness of God's life. Universalism, and I am speaking in general, upholds the view that image restored is the full package when in fact both design (image restored) and identity (agreeing with that image) in harmony, is the ultimate. What's the difference? Well let's say we have two people.

A wealthy man comes along and deposits a large amount of money in both their bank accounts. He then sends both a message describing what he had done. One carries on as if nothing happened, going about his daily business and the other utilizes what's been given him and enjoys a lavish life. This is the same with our innocence in Jesus. We can turn our back on it or we can grab a hold of it and enjoy His quality of life. What would be the distinguishing factor between the two people? The difference would be quality of life!

Abraham believed and it was counted to him as righteousness. What did Abraham believe? He believed that God could justify the ungodly. Abraham believed what God said about him. Does it say God would justify the ungodly with a little help from his friends or does it say He and only He would justify the ungodly? We are justified by faith when we agree that He already sees and regards us as righteous.

Paul also says that the righteous shall live by faith. Correctly translated *"live"* would read: *"have life."* So those who have been justified will enter into the quality of that very life that justified them - upon believing.

Conclusion:

God's reality about us becomes our reality when we agree with His opinion about us.

The righteous shall have life by faith.

The righteous (God's reality about us)

shall have life (becomes our reality)

by faith (when we agree with His opinion/reality about us.)

"That in the dispensation of the fulness of times he might gather together in one all things in Christ, both which are in heaven, and which are on earth; even in him"
Ephesians 1:10 KJV

So if God placed me in Christ without my participation, then what is left for me to do? I'm sorted right? No, not really. In fact, this happened to everyone. How everyone acts on that makes all the difference. You see being placed in Christ is a big deal otherwise we wouldn't have a proper platform from which to relate to our Father but, ...and here it comes - you need to accept it and make an already reality with God, YOUR REALITY by faith. You need to believe it.

Innocence or inclusion is objective salvation. More on this in comparison to subjective salvation later. The finished work is Him making us righteous. The finished work is His job. Our job is to agree and enjoy it.

CHAPTER 4
UNDERSTANDING GOD'S GRACE

*"This then is the message which we have heard of him,
and declare unto you, that God is light, and in him is
no darkness at all." 1 John 1:5 KJV*

This message Jesus brings, is unadulterated and puts God on show for who He really is. We will look at the first couple of chapters of Genesis with this perspective. I would like to call it a grace perspective but it would not be scripturally correct. Grace and truth only came with Jesus Christ as the gospel of John says. But Christ (the Word) was part of the Trinity, with the Father, from before creation you might add. Rightly so, I agree grace existed then, but it could only be visible by the Word concerning us, becoming flesh.

" 1 In the beginning was the Word, and the Word was with God, and the Word was God. 2 The same was in the beginning with God. 3 All things were made by him; and without him was not any thing made that was made." John 1:1-3 KJV

*"And the **Word** was made flesh, and dwelt among us, (and we beheld his glory, the glory as of the only begotten of the Father,) **full of grace and truth.**"* John 1:14 KJV

*"25 Then he said unto them, O fools, and slow of heart to believe all that the prophets have spoken: 26 Ought not Christ to have suffered these things, and to enter into his glory? 27 And **beginning** at **Moses** and all the **prophets**, he expounded unto them in all the scriptures the things **concerning himself.**"*
Luke 24:25-27 KJV

Moses in this verse refers to Moses' writings. Considering all of the above verses we see that grace existed right from the beginning but could only be visible in the incarnation of Jesus Christ.

A moral dilemma

Grace had a bad rap right from the word go. He came unto His own and they received Him not. Remember that verse? I cannot even begin to explain my disdain when someone discovered I'm in a grace church and the first thing they manage to utter is something along the lines of: *"Oh, so you give people a license to sin?"* or *"Oh, so you do as you like?"* or my favorite: *"So you just do nothing?"*

First of all. People have been sinning without a license for ages so you are not making any sense. Grace does not inspire you to sin. You are confusing grace with the law, because you want to reason it out from a law perspective which is a feeble attempt to say the least. The apostle Paul makes it very clear that the law is the power of sin. And secondly. No, that's your mentality not mine. Funny how Jesus exposes your heart as soon as you are confronted with His truth. He is the embodiment of grace after all. You are showing me that you are living a life of obligation and not of relationship. Your Christianity is a chore and your spiritual life is not the result of the influence of God, being led by the Spirit, but rather rule keeping. I have a question for you if you have this mentality. Let's say you are happily married and you have everything to be fulfilled in every aspect of your lives. What is the chance of you saying?: *"I can't wait to sneak off and get a hooker!"* No? Do you see what mentality you are stuck with? If that's you then there is something seriously wrong. That is not a relationship mindset. That is messed up proper.

Here's another one. Let's say you are the proud owner of a brand new V16 Rolls Royce Phantom. Would it make any sense for you to lust after a rust-bucket VW Beetle, sporting a paint-job that resembles a partially digested piece of candy? My guess is that you won't. So why this attitude towards grace. Simply because grace is misunderstood. We tend to attack that which we don't know. The same is true in relating to God. The reason being this: Yes, you guessed it. Christianity barely knows Him. Just like the time Jesus appeared in John 1 and His own received Him not, likewise His message is frowned upon by the religious status quo today. And thirdly. Rest is not to be confused with passivity. So no. I am not doing nothing. I operate from a place of rest. Huge difference between that and .... just doing nothing. I was always intrigued by the accusation of being passive and I could never understand as to why people viewed rest as passivity. Then it dawned on me as I watched the movie - Amazing Grace. A slave has no reference to rest. So when a slave then sees someone doing nothing, his rule of thumb kicks in, and his first thought would be that the person is lazy or passive. As soon as you take the self effort out of the message as you present grace, the legalist comes to life and defends the faith, or rather that which he perceives to be the faith.

I heard a TV-preacher say that the purpose of the law was to legislate morality, and then it dawned on me. The whole issue law preachers have with grace believers is a morality issue. This would imply that if a person refrains from *"keeping"* the law, they would automatically be regarded as immoral. Years ago, when I revealed to a friend that I was an atheist, his first question was: *"On what do you base your morality?"* to which my response was a tad uncalled for as I was lacking the fruit of the Spirit back then. But you get the point. To the law mind, anything outside of abiding by the law of Moses is out of bounds and off limits. So we as grace believers are judged as immoral beings when the contrary is in fact true. Although I was not a believer at the time, without the law of Moses I was regarded as immoral. What utter nonsense!

I agree that there are moral stuff in the law but don't get me wrong, the law was never to be solely a moral compass. The law was given to show man's incapability to please God and to point man back to God who is the only one who can fulfill it. It's not a good thing to judge people's morality when you don't know them from a bar of soap.

Grace is the influence of God on the heart of man. When you are a believer in Jesus, His seed inside you bears fruit (morals) etc. See - the fruit of the Spirit. And this is the only way you will ever have Godly fruit in your life. Christ is inside the believer and is supposed to be the LIFE of the believer. We don't live by a set of rules to be moral and bear fruit. The law can never bear Godly fruit! We need to trust Christ in the believer to bear Godly fruit. The law never produced a single christian. Never has, never will!

Unmerited favor?

In today's church, grace has a lot of different meanings to a lot of different people. Everyone defines it in their own way and thus live accordingly. The most common definition for grace in the church is unmerited favor. So why can't unmerited favor describe it fully? Simply because grace has very little to do with favor. **Favor** refers back to old testament mercy which is not to be confused with grace. Anyways, how do you fall from mercy when it's new every morning? Some people define it like that because the amplified bible says so and so grace has no further meaning than favor to them. To deem grace as futile we only need to give it a lame definition that discredits the true meaning which is the same as spreading untruths about it. Unmerited favor is an attempt to interpret grace from limited resources.

Grace is spiritually discerned, an acquired taste if you like.

A law or slave mindset cannot possibly define its rich spiritual meaning. Paul puts it as follows:

"13 Which things also we speak, not in the words which man's wisdom teacheth, but which the Holy Ghost teacheth; comparing spiritual things with spiritual. 14 But the natural man receiveth not the things of the Spirit of God: for they are foolishness unto him: neither can he know them, because they are spiritually discerned." 1 Corinthians 2:13-14 KJV

I call that - *"a carnal-man translation of a God (spiritual) thing."* By the way, the only man that could ever translate God fully is Jesus. Let's say you're an old testament prophet, for the sake of the illustration. You then receive a vision from God concerning the future. This vision features cars and motorcycles – things unknown to you and the time you live in. You yourself are not exactly sure what it was you saw in the vision, so when it's time to convey what you saw, you interpret and explain according to what you perceive it to be - according to what you are used to. Cars would be chariots - motorcycles would be horses. You see what I mean? Unmerited favor falls in the slave interpretation camp, but it makes perfect sense when we realize it is man trying to explain grace on the basis of a somewhat limited, God-deprived frame of reference. A religion induced inferiority complex brought on a warped definition of grace that calls it undeserved and unmerited favor.

When seen from God's perspective, unmerited doesn't make sense, even though it makes sense from our fallen view. **Unmerited** means you don't really deserve it − you have no merit. This could not be further from the truth. Grace never was and never will be undeserved. God showed grace as divine influence to show you your original design. Something you deserve! He regards it as wrong that you have to make your way through life without His quality of life! The wisdom of the serpent says you are inferior and you have to perform to receive what's already yours. Your Father is not into playing inferiority games with you. Not only is it bad PR, but it limits your potential in Him and talks down to you. As we have already established in the previous chapter on innocence, you would find it hard for someone to possess what you already possess if they don't regard themselves as your equal.

You had merit all along. You were created in His image. Jesus did not come to make you valuable − He came because you had value all along. You are the treasure in the field, the lost coin, the pearl of great price. He gave up His immortality to come find you. You were bought/redeemed with God currency. The price paid (Jesus) is equivalent to the value of the goods bought (you). Don't let anyone tell you you don't have merit or that you are worthless. That is not God speaking. That's the devil right there!

Words like unmerited favor and unconditional love cannot be found in your Father's vocabulary. It is simply not family language.

I can think of a couple examples on how unmerited favor cannot exist within the confines of a healthy family setting. When someone dear to us are in trouble, we don't treat them as undeserving or measure them up against an imaginary standard of merit. On the contrary, we would treat them as having merit with us and worthy of our help. When my wife called me one late afternoon, informing me there's something wrong with the car, I did not first do a merit-check on her to see if she's worthy of my assistance. When she breaks down (runs out of fuel) - I break down (I run out of fuel) whether I like it or not. Me treating her as anything other than my equal – telling her she doesn't have merit would only worsen the situation. Of course she has merit. She is bone of my bones and flesh of my flesh. We are one. If I mistreat her, I mistreat myself. You catch my drift?

So the next time you find yourself in a situation where one of your loved one's are in desperate need your help. Try this. Tell them they don't really deserve your help but you'll do it anyway. You would *"unmerited favor"* them in other words. Do you think they would ask you for help again? Let me know how that works out for you. I can only imagine my wife's facial expression if I tried a stunt like that. I'd probably get a well deserved kick up the backside. When unmerited favor enters through the front door - grace (family) is out the back door. This is due to the fact that they are opposites. Unmerited favor cannot even be mentioned in the same breath as grace. Some on the other hand say it's only a gift as noted in Ephesians 2:8

"For by grace are ye saved through faith; and that not of yourselves: it is the gift of God." Ephesians 2:8 KJV

I agree that grace is a gift. This verse can be likened to John 3:16

"For God so loved the world, that he gave his only begotten Son, that whosoever believeth in him should not perish, but have everlasting life." John 3:16 KJV

*"For by grace........it is the **gift** of God."*
*"He **gave** His only begotten......."*

Jesus is the gift. He is the influence God wants to have on us. If we lose the true meaning of grace it will have no effect on us.

"For the law was given by Moses, but grace and truth came by Jesus Christ." John 1:17 KJV

Grace is God in human form.

Backsliding

Backsliding is returning to the law after being presented with grace. I have found that those who warn against grace haven't experienced it for themselves. Either that or they have a warped definition for grace. Some warn about the great falling away in the last days. If you want to quote Paul to justify your end-time deception theory in an attempt to incriminate grace, remember this:

You cannot backslide TO grace - you backslide FROM grace back TO the law. If you don't believe me you can read the whole epistle Paul wrote to the Galatians. In this particular epistle he addresses the church in Galatia, who had fallen prey to the law-spreading gang and returned to observing the law. These law preachers are also the thorn in Paul's flesh, which he describes elsewhere. Paul never warned anyone against grace. It would be like someone putting his own life on the line for what he believes and then warn you against it. That would be very destructive to one's ministry to say the least.

To say that Paul warned against grace is ludicrous and it would make Paul out to be a really stupid person. We know the contrary to be true. Paul was in fact more learned than most law preachers today. He calls the Galatians foolish for turning their backs on the good news (grace) and returning to works of the law.

Hyper grace

Although I am not particularly fond of this term, seeing that it was coined by a law preacher who knows nothing about grace, I respond with all courteousness and take it as a compliment. Here's why. Calling the message I adhere to as *"hyper"* you are subconsciously and automatically admitting that my message is superior to yours. If you label the grace I preach as *"hyper"* grace - Is your grace mediocre? Is it sub-standard grace? Is it not so hyper? Is it the sort of grace you would rather keep to yourself because you're scared it would make others miserable also, like it did you?

I refrain from using the term as I view it as just another cause for confusion in the body. Its initial purpose was to be destructive to the message of grace.

A common occurrence among theologians is to make such an effort to oppose a view different from theirs, that they forgot what they themselves believed and stood for.

One day we were driving to the city and I noticed a bumper sticker on an old Land Rover. It read: *"I would rather push a Landy than drive Jap-Crap."* This is exactly what's wrong in some theological circles today. Because of our pride, we would rather promote and make our theology work by our own efforts, than adhere to something that works, or in the case of the car, something that runs and gives good mileage on fuel. Something that actually gets us from point A to point B. We would rather push a piece of crap that depleted our life savings, than settle for something that actually runs and functions properly. Grace runs perfectly without your effort. Just call it grace.

So why does Paul call it the following?

huperperisseuo – over, above, beyond + superabounding riches (Romans 5:20)

huperballo – over, above, beyond + to throw beyond (Ephesians 2:7)

huperpleonazo – over, above, beyond + to increase, superabound (1 Timothy 1:14)

Grace is *"hyper"* because the incarnation of Jesus in human flesh is over, above and beyond any influence we could conjure up in a mortal body, utilizing the wisdom of the serpent - trying to keep the law.

Grace as divine influence

The one definition that is usually neglected, is the one that makes the most sense of all. We have a habit of neglecting that which we do not understand. Grace as an influence. You see the very same mentality that attacks the grace believer's morality, still possesses a very much alive, old man complex.

*"What shall we say then? **Shall we continue in sin,** that grace may abound? 2 God forbid. How shall we, that are **dead to sin,** live any longer therein? 3 Know ye not, that so many of us as were baptized into Jesus Christ were **baptized into his death?** 4 Therefore we are buried with him by baptism into death: that like as Christ was raised up from the dead by the glory of the Father, even so we also should walk in newness of life. 5 For if we have been planted together in the likeness of his death, we shall be also in the likeness of his resurrection: 6 Knowing this, that our **old man is crucified with him,** that the body of sin might be destroyed, that henceforth we should not serve sin. 7 For he that is dead is freed from sin."*
Romans 6:1-7 KJV

Here we have Paul addressing that very same mentality. People that don't know they were included. The goal of their christianity is to put the old man to death or starve him by exercising empowering, unmerited favor when our point of departure in our christian walk starts off with this advantage. Our **old man** is already **dead!** You being placed in Christ was not a result of your faith but rather in order for you to believe. To remain in Him is up to you! (see John 15) I am of the opinion that if we don't fully grasp our inclusion in the death, burial, resurrection and ascension of Jesus to the Father's right hand as discussed in the previous chapter, we won't fully grasp grace. Our inclusion in Christ is exactly the influence God wants to have on us. This is probably the best definition to describe the Father's heart. Grace as an influence describes His character. It describes Him as a gentleman. No pushing or shoving towards you to get to know Him or in bearing fruit. Only a gentle gesture toward Jesus who represents us.

Grace was not known to man before Jesus. Grace is God in a human body. First in the body of Jesus and then in the body of the believer. Let's say you are approaching someone's property. This property is unfortunately guarded by a bad tempered dog. Would you have the confidence to approach and let yourself in by the front gate? Probably not. Because the dog has an influence on you not to come any closer. This dog has a "word" concerning himself and the property. That word is: *"You will endure pain on entering here."* He is influencing you to stay away. Likewise and on a better note, Jesus is the embodiment of the Father's influence on us. Jesus is the invitation from the Father, the Word concerning us. He shows us that the throne room of our Father is not a restricted area as we were taught. He shows us our design. As soon as we see our design, it aides us toward its companion – identity.

Grace
G5485 Strong's
charis

: especially the **divine influence** upon the **heart**, and its **reflection** in the life.

God became man so He could **influence** man. He had to become something we can relate to. In carrying our sin He could then relate to our condition. God knows exactly how you feel in your darkest hour. Remember the sin of the whole world was on Him at the cross. This reminds me of the homeless man that was given pizza on that youtube video. A couple of guys did a social experiment approaching random people in restaurants and even on the streets asking them for food. They claimed to be starving of course. None of the people they approached gave them anything, some barely noticed them. Later on in a park they came across a homeless man sitting next to his shopping cart filled with all his belongings. They gave him a fresh pizza and left. Cameras still pointed at the homeless man, he opened the pizza box had a slice or two and closed it again. A couple of minutes later another guy pretending to be hungry, and also part of the experiment, approached the homeless man and asked whether he had any food. Without any hesitation the homeless man reached over to the pizza box and offered him some pizza. This brought tears to my eyes. Firstly seeing how desensitized our society had become and secondly how a man that has nothing, a man that doesn't even know where his next meal would come from, shares his food with a total stranger. You see, this man knows what it's like to be hungry and he could completely relate to someone else who claims to be hungry. In this same manner Jesus came in the form of man, subject to the system in which man found himself in order to redeem man from that system.

Say for instance He came as anything other than a human. How much credibility would he then have with humans? Not much I guess. God would have sadly remained non-relatable.

The Incarnation is Key

The incarnation of God in human form is key in understanding grace. In our day we see this horrendous attack on the divinity of Jesus and hence nullifying the very act that He proposes to mankind. The act of influence.

This creation is crying out for the manifestation of the sons of God while the church leaders are playing church-church in someone's backyard debating the divinity of Jesus and other silly crap. Jesus will have no influence on you when you only regard Him as a mere man. We will discuss influence in depth in a while.

Nowadays so many a westerner, flock to the east for

spiritual enlightenment, to yet again bow to images of monkeys with seven tails or an elephant with three trunks, whilst calling christianity absurd. I know, I know. The church is partly to blame. I am not trying to mock someone else's religion I am trying to make sense of it. Family sense. Trinity sense. A Father relating to His children sense. I mean, how on earth can I relate to a monkey or an elephant. We are still stuck with creatures and not the Creator. I cannot relate to a monkey or an elephant. The monkey does not know how I feel. There can be limited affection but no fellowship. They simply cannot relate to my human condition. I can sympathize to their condition and take care of them being a higher creature myself, but I don't want a God I have to take care of, if you know what I mean. So that's out of the question. They will never know what it is to be me, they cannot relate to my pain, laugh about something silly or ultimately take away my sin. This is what makes our God different. He becomes a man.

You see God never knew what it was like to be a man until He incarnated Himself into Jesus. He had to take on the likeness of fallen man to be able to redeem man. He can fully empathize with you because he knows exactly how you feel. All your bad experiences, sickness and shortcomings but to name a few. He had to accept our condition to relate to us one on one. He loves us so much that He got His hands dirty to get the job done right. The creator of the heavens and the earth cares so much about you that He became a man to carry that which was too heavy for you.

One evening I was flicking through the channels on the decoder. You know, one of those evenings when there's nothing to watch on the telly. I came across a BBC channel, and having lived in England for a couple of years, I grew quite fond of their culture and sense of humor. Showing on that channel was a series called Downton Abbey. The series, set in the fictional Yorkshire country estate of Downton Abbey, depicts the lives of the aristocratic Crawley family and their domestic servants in the post-Edwardian era - with the great events in history having an effect on their lives and on the British social hierarchy.

In this particular episode, one could clearly see the social hierarchy of the day. His lordship and her ladyship would be sipping tea in the great hall along with their high society friends. In contrast with that picture you would have the servants shining shoes, ironing clothes and going about the daily chores of such a huge household. Some days I wouldn't mind living that sort of life, you know, but unfortunately I would be bored out of my scull. Back to the episode. His lordship, the owner, and the head butler had a conversation and the butler addressed his lordship as *"my lord."* Then it hit me. *"That guy ain't no lord!"* I thought to myself. I immediately knew what was wrong with this picture. You see Jesus has redefined the word Lord to me and you in order for us to better understand Him. He shows us in Matthew 23:11 the true definition of *"Lord"*.

"But he that is greatest among you shall be your servant."
Matthew 23:11 KJV

While pondering on this verse and looking at our injustice towards, and twisting of the meaning, this question came to me: *"How do one serve a servant?"* At this point in my life it was nothing new to me having God speak to me through a tv-show. Once a prophetess visiting our church said: *"God cannot speak to you if you're watching television!"* Ever since that day He has proven the contrary. He can even speak to you on the loo you know. Let's not go there. *"How do one serve a servant?"* There it was again. *"What do you mean?"* I asked. *"My Son came to serve man, right?"* He replied. *"Yes, indeed!"* I replied. He continued: *"So in the light of what you see on the telly; how would you suppose his lordship would have to go about in serving the butler?"* I was looking for an answer and what came to mind in this domestic situation at hand was this: *"I would try to make his work-load substantially lighter."* For example: *"One could help with the chores in and around the house."* Not to bad for a rapid comeback, I thought. *"Would it be of much help if the servant was born in you rather?"* He asked. I was speechless and knew grace was so misunderstood, and still is. He continued: *"You would have to let the servant do what He does best, that is, to serve you, then spend time with Him and get to know His heart."*

We need Jesus to serve us first so we can see His heart, His feelings towards us. It is almost like: We love Him because He first loved us. We can only love when we experience how much we are loved. Likewise we can only serve when we experience how we are being served by Him. To put it plainly. His burden becomes our burden. His caring for the lost become our caring for the lost. His emotions become our emotions. What's important to Him becomes important to us. Jesus is the greatest servant of all time. He never hesitated on getting His hands dirty to get the job done proper. He came as a servant to show us the Father and changed the definition of *"Lord"* forever.

This God-life is not driven by commandments and rules. Grace is the influence of God on the belief system of man and manifested in the life of that very man. What man believes will be evident in his actions. When grace is understood a lot of things would fall into place automatically. Giving would become influence based and not reward based. Humility would come naturally and wouldn't need fasting and prayer to induce it. Yes, you know who you are! Ministry would be ministering to God's people and less of a competitive sport. When grace is misunderstood we want to make it work. When it is an influence it comes natural.

Do you think a guy that got hammered in a bar on whiskey needs to work on his act to look drunk? No. He's under the influence, he is not in control anymore. The whiskey is!

Grace as empowerment

"Knowledge is power." - Sir Francis Bacon

We have already established that it is a natural response for a law-saturated mind to automatically revert back to a works default when confronted with truth of rather in this case, grace. So when the law mind is introduced to grace as an empowerment, it wants do do something – it just has to do something. Thus grace as an empowerment is reduced to God empowering you to keep the law. He saw you could not do it, so He empowered you to keep it. Believe it or not this is a widely accepted belief regarding grace. Only one problem with that. The law could never give you the Spirit. The law could not produce a single christian. Never has, never will. It was never intended to do that in the first place. So if God empowers you to keep the law, He's in actual fact sending you around in circles and never enjoying His life. That just doesn't sound like Him. The God I've come to know wants for everyone to know Him – not sending them on a wild goose chase. (a foolish and hopeless search for, or pursuit of something unattainable.)

Grace as an empowerment needs to be rooted firmly in divine influence, otherwise it would only result in yet another *"how to"* or *"DIY"* principle you need to work. So how does divine influence work in practice. God reaches us on our level with His grand view concerning us. He becomes a man. He divinely influenced us with the incarnation of Jesus in human flesh. Jesus is His human agent. Still is today.

*"For the law was given by Moses, but **grace** and **truth** came by **Jesus Christ**."* John 1:17 KJV

Surveying the truth about us in Jesus empowers us. Simple as that. An empowerment to do what? I always ask. You see it is easy to fall back into the slave mentality and translate grace as an empowerment as a means by which to try keep the law. Paul describes being subject to the law as being without strength.

*"For when we were yet without **strength**, in due time Christ died for the ungodly."* Romans 5:6 KJV

We were in the dark concerning God's opinion about us, so to speak, and that in itself rendered us powerless. As soon as we see God's opinion about us in the light of the incarnation of Jesus we are empowered.

*"2 **Grace** and peace be **multiplied** unto you through the **knowledge** of God, and of Jesus our Lord, 3 According as his divine **power** hath given unto us all things that pertain unto life and godliness, through the **knowledge** of him that hath called us to glory and virtue: 4 Whereby are given unto us exceeding great and precious promises: that by these ye might be partakers of the divine nature, having escaped the corruption that is in the world through lust."* 2 Peter 1:2-4 KJV

76

Here Peter shows us how grace is directly connected to the knowledge of God displayed in the incarnation and how it works to empower us. **Knowledge** of God, shown in Jesus as grace (divine influence) **is power.**

*"9 And he said unto me, My **grace** is sufficient for thee: for my **strength** is made perfect in weakness. Most gladly therefore will I rather glory in my infirmities, that the **power of Christ** may rest upon me. 10 Therefore I take pleasure in infirmities, in reproaches, in necessities, in persecutions, in distresses for Christ's sake: for when I am weak, then am I strong."*
2 Corinthians 12:9-10 KJV

Paul was also well aware of the fact that grace is the power of God, even more so than Peter. Here he shows us how we, on hearing the good news gets empowered unto salvation. That is because the good news about us. The truth about us as shown in Jesus.

*"For I am not ashamed of the **gospel** of Christ: for it is the **power** of God unto salvation to every one that **believeth**; to the Jew first, and also to the Greek."* Romans 1:16 KJV

*"For when we were yet without **strength**, in due time Christ died for the ungodly."* Romans 5:6 KJV

The good news is Christ died our death. We were without strength that is, not knowing who we were to God and any attempt to die away our old man would have been futile because under law we had no promise of the resurrection of the dead. He came to do it on our behalf as us with the promise that the Father would raise Him from the dead. Him as our representative is our strength or in other words, we survey Him and His finished work and we are empowered unto godliness. When we believe (agree with God), we are empowered to enjoy His quality of life.

Grace is not a movement

The life of the believer can be likened to a journey God takes us on, to His original intent with us. On this road-trip, some allow Him to influence them with His goodness and His life, so they sit back in His rest. They operate from this position. His peace is the governing factor in everything they put their hand to. This rest is not to be confused with passivity.

Some on the other hand get distracted by the *"signs"* beside the road while others are more bothered with what they were given to drive. Signs can go both ways, from feeling blessed by the scenery to feeling cursed by a flat tyre. Some take pride in and are consumed with the Rolls Royce they were *"entrusted"* with and some discontent with the VW beetle they were *"entrusted" with. Meanwhile both will get to the destination. The key is to be content. Unfortunately the "signs and wonders"* en-route and the *"vehicle"* (financial prosperity or the lack thereof) becomes distractions and some get preoccupied with them. This is the breeding ground and birthplace of MOVEMENTS. This is also where the wheels come off the glorified prosperity gospel, posing as the message of grace. The reason for this is simple. You cannot preach a prosperity gospel and then go on to tell the hearers to be content with what they have been entrusted with, simultaneously. I have nothing against prosperity at all. Your financial prosperity or the lack thereof should not have a voice concerning your identity. There's a lot of rich people out there – and all some of them have is money!

Movements lack the ability to define Jesus. Grace puts the destination, the signs and the vehicle in perspective and fully define Jesus. Jesus says the thief came to steal kill and destroy but He came that we could have life and have it more abundantly. Life to deal with anything the world throws at you and then that very life overflows into eternal life – the destination, so to speak. This destination is not us trying to work out our salvation, it is Him giving our flesh immortality in His return. He is influencing us unto immortality. Our salvation is His doing start to finish. We participate by believing it.

"To whom God would make known what is the riches of the glory of this mystery among the Gentiles; which is Christ in you, the hope of glory:" Colossians 1:27 KJV

God influences us with the incarnation of Jesus. When we believe this message, that very influence becomes our influence. Christ living in the human being. Jesus at the right hand of God is God's view and opinion of all of mankind. He holds all of mankind in high esteem. That influences us to draw near resulting in us having Christ in us. Christ in us is the hope of the manifestation of the sons (immortality). Grace is not a movement, it's a message. A God-message wrapped up in human flesh, addressed to you and me.

PART 3
THE GARDEN IN THE LIGHT OF GRACE

CHAPTER 5
CREATION

"In the beginning God created the heavens and the earth."
Genesis 1:1 KJV

Looking at this very first verse of the bible in the Hebrew, the word *"created"* actually means complete and perfect as it is accompanied by the mysterious untranslated phrase, marked (H853-Strong's) which means *"aleph-tav."* Alpha-Omega in simpler terms. The Message translation talks about the seen and the unseen. The heavens as unseen and the earth as the seen, per se. Taking all these facts and translations in consideration my translation of verse one would be: *"In the beginning God created the the earth to reflect His reality by means of His Word - Alpha-Omega (Christ.)*

"And the earth was without form, and void; and darkness was upon the face of the deep. And the Spirit of God moved upon the face of the waters." Genesis 1:2 KJV

The very first thought that comes to mind is that these two verses are contradictory. Rightly so. Let us take a closer look. It may seem that God created this chaotic earth. But the original language comes to our aid. Let us dissect this verse and process it properly. The word **was** in the phrase "....and the earth **was** without form.." is translated **"hayah"** which means **had become**. So God created the earth complete and perfect but it **had become** without form and void. And darkness was upon the face of the deep. And the Spirit of God moved upon the face of the waters.

The earth had become void, uninhabited. The inhabitants were all subject to death and subsequently succumbed to the *"death-life"* that was at the order of the day. That *"death-life"* is the result of the wisdom of the serpent in religion. Relating to God in a self righteous, works oriented manner. That can only lead to death. Someone must have been responsible for this and looking at this scene from a finished work perspective we know all too well. Some scholars are of the opinion that the original earth, or as we will refer to it here as Earth 1, was subject to a cataclysmic event called the flood of Lucifer. Almost like the flood of Noah but on a much bigger scale. Noah's flood was limited to a specific area whereas the flood of Lucifer covered the whole earth and thus caused complete destruction. No inhabitants left and a complete mess.

".... and the Spirit of God moved upon the face of the waters." This here is one of those scriptures that has been intriguing me since I first read it. What could it mean? The Spirit of God is translated here in different ways but one makes more sense to the topic at hand.

Spirit
Brown Driver Briggs Definition

1d) spirit (of the living, breathing being in man and animals) 1d1) as gift, preserved by God, God's spirit, departing at death, disembodied being.

So God's Spirit was moving on the face of the waters as a disembodied being. The earth was uninhabited on account of the flood and thus the Spirit of God had no one to inhabit on that earth. It also makes perfect sense to say then that God wasn't part of the mess. Spirit is also translated **exhalation** as in creation exhaling God's life. The earth basically giving up the ghost. One scripture that comes to mind is:

"And the LORD said, My spirit shall not always strive with man, for that he also is flesh: yet his days shall be an hundred and twenty years." Genesis 6:3 KJV

This may also have been the case prior to the destruction of Earth 1. For clarity I will refer to the earth in Genesis 1:1 as **Earth 1**, Genesis 1:2 as **Earth 2** and our current earth, the one we read about in the creation story as **Earth 3**.

Earth 1	Gap	Earth 2	Earth 3
Genesis 1:1	Fall of Lucifer	Genesis 1:2	Genesis 1:3 (subject to decay)
Perfect Creation	Destruction of Earth 1 Flood of Lucifer	Fallen Creation prior to the creation story starting at Genesis 1:3	Repaired creation
Light and darkness separate	Corrupted	Light and darkness mixed	Light and darkness separate

The gap theory

There exists the stance in theological circles called the gap theory. In short the gap theory states the existence of a gap between Genesis 1:1 and Genesis 1:2. A period of time not stated by the author of the book of Genesis but visible when we consider God's integrity of character in the creation story. Why does the author endorse the gap theory? The simple explanation for this is the mere fact that the gap theory proves God to be good. He is not the author of **without form** and **void**. Either you believe God created the mess as stated in Genesis 1:2 and you have a messed up theology or you believe God to be good and that He created the earth good and it had become chaotic and dark on account of a different influence.

"Through faith we understand that the worlds were framed by the word of God, so that things which are seen were not made of things which do appear." Hebrews 11:3 KJV

The word **framed** is **katartizo** in the greek and translated, repair, mend and restore among others. This explains the gap theory. That God made Earth 1 perfect and complete, it got corrupted and succumbed to the influence of Lucifer resulting in Earth 2, the one we read about in Genesis 1:2. God steps onto the scene again as restorer and recreates earth to the state it is in at the creation story. That is the third state of the earth. Earth 3. See diagram.

The fall of Lucifer

*"12 How art thou fallen from heaven , O **Lucifer**, son of the morning! How art thou **cut down** to the ground, which didst weaken the nations! 13 For thou hast said in thine heart, I will ascend into heaven, I will exalt my throne above the stars of*

*God: I will sit also upon the mount of the congregation, in the sides of the north: 14 I will ascend above the heights of the clouds; I will be like the most High. 15 Yet thou shalt be brought down to hell, to the sides of the pit. 16 They that see thee shall narrowly look upon thee and consider thee, saying, is this the man that made the earth to tremble, that did shake kingdoms; 17 That made the world as a **wilderness**, and **destroyed** the cities thereof; that opened not the house of his prisoners?"*
Isaiah 14:12-17 KJV

The fall of Lucifer as described in this piece of scripture clearly points out the culprit responsible for the devastation of Earth 1.

"I have made him fair by the multitude of his branches: so that all the trees of Eden, that were in the garden of God, envied him." Ezekiel 31:9 KJV

"To whom art thou thus like in glory and in greatness among the trees of Eden? yet shalt thou be brought down with the trees of Eden unto the nether parts of the earth: thou shalt lie in the midst of the uncircumcised with them that be slain by the sword. This is Pharaoh and all his multitude, saith the Lord GOD."
Ezekiel 31:18 KJV.

In the preceding two verses Lucifer is likened unto a tree. The planting of the Lord. Likewise believers are also referred to as trees of righteousness. As trees planted by the waters.

"For he shall be as a tree planted by the waters, and that spreadeth out her roots by the river, and shall not see when heat cometh, but her leaf shall be green; and shall not be careful in the year of drought, neither shall cease from yielding fruit."
Jeremiah 17:8 KJV

"Thou hast been in Eden the garden of God; every precious stone was thy covering, the sardius, topaz, and the diamond, the beryl, the onyx, and the jasper, the sapphire, the emerald, and

the carbuncle, and gold: the workmanship of thy tabrets and of thy pipes was prepared in thee in the day that thou wast created." Ezekiel 28:13 KJV

"The workmanship of thy tabrets and of thy pipes was prepared in thee ...." describes God's purpose for him, Lucifer, best. His original state was the workmanship of God. He was created to praise God. To show forth the righteousness of God. God doing the right thing towards His creation. God prepared/established him for this purpose. The sole purpose of his existence was to enjoy God's provision, His sustenance and glory and then ascribe all the attributes of the Godhead back to God. He was to be a living showcase of the goodness of God. He is also likened to a tree that was planted by God. We will see a bit more of that tree in the chapter on the tree of knowledge of good and evil. God did not plant a bad tree in the garden of Eden to test man. That is probably the biggest lie ever told. This implies that man is inherently evil and that God creates evil which could according to the creation story not be further from the truth. The creation story tells us that after every day of creation, God said ....it was GOOD! When creatures turn bad it's on their own account of giving in to the wrong influence. This is also the case with Lucifer/the tree of knowledge of good and evil. He was the planting of the Lord, but in stead of ascribing God's attributes back to Him, Lucifer wanted to keep the praise and the glory to himself. Even ascribing his Creator's sustenance and provision to himself. His wisdom became corrupted when God was left out of his equation. Will you look at the arrogance! Talk about biting the hand that feeds you.

Now considering this criteria surrounding Lucifer we can see how **Earth 1** probably had the same basic layout as

Earth 3 in the creation story.

Lucifer means *"bearer of light"*. Light speaks of the Word or message of God concerning something. His job description also implied affirming God's Word. God creates everything in **Earth 1** exactly the same, by His Word. Lucifer comes along and mixes God's light/message with his message/word concerning creation. This caused the corruption of the good message of God in **Earth 1** resulting in the devastation we see in **Earth 2**. The message concerning God had become one of mixture. This light was a mixture of light and darkness. Remember the Spirit of God moved upon the face of the waters. God's Spirit had no part in that mess.

Lucifer had freedom of choice to ascribe to God the attributes that were due to Him, but he rather ascribed it to himself which resulted in the corruption of his own wisdom. Lucifer became his own god and this became the system we know as the tree of knowledge of good and evil which was also later written down in stone.

God takes the initiative to bear fruit in and through His creation. As soon as you succumb to Lucifer's influence you would ascribe God's fruit-bearing to yourself, simultaneously cutting God off and the end result will be you being deprived of His life and being subject to death.

Let there be light

"3 And God said, Let there be light: and there was light. 4 And God saw the light, that it was good: and God divided the light from the darkness. 5 And God called the light Day, and the darkness he called Night. And the evening and the morning were the first day." Genesis 1:3-5 KJV

Similar to the creation story in genesis, John the Apostle kicks off with *"In the beginning..."*

In this chapter we will see the importance of having a perspective from a finished work and to be established in who God is and what His intentions are. *"Let there be light"* cannot be interpreted unless we have background on who that light is. God was clearly not speaking of creating the sun when He said: *"Let there be light."* The sun was created on the fourth day. So what was God talking about?

Let us take a closer look to what God means with this statement in the light of the new testament. God stays exactly the same. John 1 explains that original intent.

"1 In the beginning was the Word, and the Word was with God, and the Word was God. 2 The same was in the beginning with God. 3 All things were made by him; and without him was not any thing made that was made. 4 In him was life; and the life was the light of men. 5 And the light shineth in darkness; and the darkness comprehended it not. 6 There was a man sent from God, whose name was John. 7 The same came for a witness, to bear witness of the Light, that all men through him might believe. 8 He was not that Light, but was sent to bear witness of that Light. 9 That was the true Light, which lighteth every man that cometh into the world." John 1:1-9 KJV

"Let there be light" should not be seen as God creating His Word or His Light. The Word was with Him right from the start. John 1. It is clear who this light is and verse one shows us the Word was God. God is not creating His word on the first day but rather puts things in the right perspective as if to say – If I'm going to do this, it will be done according to this standard. The standard of His creative force. His Word. At the start of the creation story we have a fallen chaotic creation of which God has no part. He introduces the fallen creation to His perfect reference point to which He measures everything – the man Jesus Christ! As if to say: Fallen creation of Genesis 1:2, meet my Word, Christ. He will sort

you out and get you on the right standard.

In *"Let there be light"* God reintroduces fallen creation to His creative, restorative Word. And by this Word/Standard He creates everything which leads to His response after each day of creation *".....and God saw that it was good."*

Light can be seen as His Word or message. The message or word about God on the fallen creation was one of mixture. This mixture word/message was the cause for the fallen creation. There was no distinction between light and darkness before God stepped onto the scene. It was as if the two were one and the same thing. The same entity. There was no night and day. When good and evil mix we get the norm that we had in the second state of the earth, exactly the same as that which the tree of knowledge of good and evil advocates. Remember Him being light and in Him is no darkness at all? So in the midst of this mixture He sets the standard and makes a distinction between the two. All of this is almost like God whispering to His creation, reminding it of its original state. The original state it had been in before the fall. The state of Genesis 1:1. Let us take it a bit closer to home. Closer and more personal to man and God's intention with man. The way God relates to something in its fallen state is exactly this. He introduces or rather reintroduces it to its original state. The way He views it. He relates to us, His people in this very same way. He approaches fallen man by showing man His intention. Jesus is His Word concerning man. In the book of Acts we see the story of Stephen. At the end of his life before he was put to death by the religion of the day, the bible says Stephen saw something.

"55 But he, being full of the Holy Ghost, looked up steadfastly into heaven, and saw the glory of God, and Jesus standing on the right hand of God, 56 And said, Behold, I see the

heavens opened, and the Son of man standing on the right hand of God." Acts 7:55-56 KJV

Verse 55 states that Stephen saw Jesus at the right hand of God, but in verse 56 he says *"the Son of man"* thus indicating the interpretation of what he saw. He understood something that very little of the new testament writers understood. Stephen saw a man in the Trinity. Jesus at the right hand of the Father speaks about God's opinion of man. God achieved this through the incarnation to show us our original design. Stephen's vision of a man in the Godhead was the light or truth of God to the hearers. In this case these were the very guys who thought they had the light. Let there be light is the proclamation of the gospel. Let there be light is God restoring His good creation to default, including you!

"3 All things were made by him; and without him was not any thing made that was made. 4 In him was life; and the life was the light of men." John 1:3-4 KJV

Jesus' life sheds light into our hearts. He shows us the love the Father has towards us. He is not merely an employee of the company, like a public relations officer trying to keep the public happy and off the back of management. He is the company. What you see with Him is what you get with the Father. He and His Father are one. Stephen saw the restoration of God and man in one vision and it would be a while before Paul grasped the power of representation.

"That was the true Light, which lighteth every man that cometh into the world."
John 1:8 KJV

"Thy word is a lamp unto my feet, and a light unto my path"
Psalm 119:105 KJV

Jesus is the lamp that shows us our original design, the way the Father sees us. When we see ourselves the way the Father sees us we can approach Him with confidence. Here's how Paul explains it.

"19 Having therefore, brethren, boldness to enter into the holiest by the blood of Jesus, 20 By a new and living way, which he hath consecrated for us, through the veil, that is to say, his flesh; 21 And having an high priest over the house of God;"
Hebrews 10:19-21 KJV

We have a High Priest representing us in the Trinity. At the right hand of the Father. God's intention with us is on an open display. That gives us confidence to approach Him and on approaching Him we can participate in His very life. *"Let there be light"* implies God entering our dark, lost condition and sheds light on us and Himself. What is true for the creation story is true for mankind.

"That in the dispensation of the fulness of times he might gather together in one all things in Christ, both which are in heaven, and which are on earth; even in him:"
Ephesians 1:10 KJV

God resets man to his original state of innocence in Christ. *"It sure doesn't look like that when I look at the world. I can clearly see that not all people know this, let alone believe it."* You might add. I agree fully. That's why it's your job to tell them. That is what we call evangelism – hello! The good news is you pointing people to Jesus who represents them with the Father. Let there be light is the beginning of restoration, seeing God's original intent!

"Let there be light" is the restoration of the message involving God, and subsequently involving man, created in His image. Jesus is this mediating light!

CHAPTER 6
IN GOD'S IMAGE

Introduction
So God made Himself an idol

Now that's a bit far fetched, don't you think? God having an idol? Let alone creating one! Even the thought of God worshiping something is taboo for most of us. Lucky for me, I don't find myself in the dark ages of church history, yet I suspect the odd attempt of resistance. When you get to know Jesus you'll find He's all about serving you. Outside of Him we have no life. The word *"image"* in the phrase *"Let us make man in Our image...."* is also translated *"idol."*

Here's how an idol functions. In the old testament the Israelites were forbidden to make themselves any carved images and bow themselves before them. An idol was traditionally made by hand, carved from stone or wood. Then this idol had to be serviced. You, the maker, has to give it life. You know, adorn it with flowers or ornaments, light a couple of candles, chuck a little perfume for fragrance, that sort of stuff. Other than your effort the idol would be lifeless. Aside from your gracious contribution it would only be another piece of wood or stone.

In this same way God made you in His image (to be His idol). He breathes life into you and you become a living soul. Just as in the case with Adam you become a living being. This has nothing to do with being filled with the Holy Spirit. This basically means you are a functioning person with the ability to reason. A living soul has a mind, will and emotions. These, when utilized, can process natural things on our journey in understanding and acquiring our identity.

In short. God creates us His Idol, one that has the ability to reason with the intention that we function like Him. To spice things up He leaves it up to us to choose our identity, you know, whether we want to resemble Him or not. He provides ample resources and influences at our disposal to make an informed decision on choosing our operating system. Almost like making a robot that looks like you with the ability to be like you but leaving the robot to choose whether he wants to be like you in terms of identity. In doing that your creation would no longer be a robot.

In the garden we find two operating systems. The wisdom of the serpent and wisdom of the fear of the Lord. In order for us to understand the original state of the *"idol"* we need to have the finished work of Jesus Christ established in our minds. This finished work perspective will shed more light on the happenings in the garden and ultimately the design and identity of man.

You and I are His handy work, taken out of Him, with the capacity to possess everything He possesses. He regards us as His equals. This sets the stage of freedom for us to enjoy His life.

In God's image

Image

H6754 Strong's

- to shade
- a phantom resemblance
- a representative
- idol

"26 And God said, Let us make man in our image, after our likeness: and let them have dominion over the fish of the sea, and over the fowl of the air, and over the cattle, and over all the earth, and over every creeping thing that creepeth upon the earth. 27 So God created man in his own image, in the image of God created he him; male and female created he them. 28 And God blessed them, and God said unto them, Be fruitful, and multiply, and replenish the earth, and subdue it: and have dominion over the fish of the sea, and over the fowl of the air, and over every living thing that moveth upon the earth."
Genesis 1:26-28 KJV

In the preceding piece of scripture we can see that God (the Trinity) decided to create man in His image and after His likeness and verse 27 goes on to say that he indeed made man in His image but then, we see no further mention of creating man after His likeness. A bit troublesome indeed at first glance, but there is an explanation for that. Let us work with what we do have at our disposal, and that being, created in his image first. What does being created in His image imply? God creates a being that operates like He does. A being that has the ability to reason and think as He does. A being that can be creative. Man is the only being that was given the ability to be like God. To rule creation as if he himself had created it. We can see this when God presents Adam with the animals to see what he would call them. Naming something means you are the owner or creator. Adam was created a very brilliant being. God created Adam with the potential to be *"like"* Him completely. Aside from being created in God's image and possessing all off these wondrous attributes of reasoning and and dealing with things on an fleshly plane, Adam was created with the capacity to contain the very life that created Him. The life of God. Adam was created with a free-will and this is exactly where agreeing with the finished work plays a role. Adam was not consulted before he was created in the state of innocence, but how Adam deals with this state he was presented with, in acknowledging his source, or rather partaking of this life is solely his choice. John 15 refers to abiding in the vine. Adam, or rather the woman was supposed to abide in what had been already done, already theirs. The reason God created man innocent is simply because He is good and He wants man to choose His life from a free-will platform void of any obligation or feeling of guilt. As we have seen earlier, guilt and condemnation are scarcely a good platform from which to start a relationship. God wants us to choose Him because we are convinced or rather persuaded of His goodness rather that the fear of torment if we don't choose Him.

God's image restored

"If you've seen Me, you've seen the Father"
- Jesus

It is very important that we have the correct image of God because that is inevitably the exact thing to which we will conform. If your Jesus is vindictive, so would your god be. And guess what? You would comply with all diligence. Do you see the cycle?

Jesus teaches people what we call the Lord's prayer and an interesting aspect to that is somehow overlooked. First of all: He tells people that are by no means *"saved"* in our terms, to address God as their Father, *"Our Father who art in heaven"* - that is speaking of our design. And secondly and equally important to this particular discussion is: *"Hallowed be Thy name."* God, as discussed earlier has had a bad rap in all areas of our lives. If it's not a natural disaster, then it's Him picking a flower when someone passes away. You see, the religious in Jesus' day tried their best to convince mankind that God was into stoning adulterers, inflicting sickness and disease on sinners, blessing good behavior, punishing bad behavior and only helping those who puts in the effort to help themselves. Can you see how the religious of Jesus' day and even in our day are advocating the tree of knowledge of good and evil? Taking part of and preaching this tree's nonsense places God in a bad light and as Jesus and Paul noted, causes the onlookers to slander God.

One of the most beautiful phrases to me is Jesus saying: *"you have heard that it was said ....but I say unto you,"* and in doing that He puts the authority of scripture in perspective. You see, we can justify almost any denomination in the history of the church by quoting scripture, but when Jesus says: *".... but I say unto you"* it is sometimes horrifying. To the humble and expectant heart this is a relief - a breath of fresh air. Like a light has been turned on in a dark room and you tell yourself: *"Man, I've always known God wasn't that petty, but now I have proof!"* Jesus is that proof. Jesus is the fullness of the Godhead in a human body. He also tells His disciples: *"If you've seen me, you've seen the Father"* and *"I only do what I see the Father do."*

Now speaking of image and design, if we are then created in God's image who do we turn to in finding out more about our design? Jesus of course! If we then present people with a warped image of God as religion does, the reference they have to find our their own design is sadly flawed. Do you see how important it is to have a right picture of God right from the start?

In the ten commandments we see God commanding the children of Israel not to make themselves any images.

"Thou shalt not make unto thee any graven image, or any likeness of any thing that is in heaven above, or that is in the earth beneath, or that is in the water under the earth:"
Exodus 20:4 KJV

My opinion is that God did not want man to try to figure out the Godhead with his limited resources. In making an image of God for themselves they would have a horizontal approach in attempting this specific task. It would be applying their earthly, vain, religious imagination in its wildest sense, making use of earthly material, something also subject to decay. Something that would need your constant maintenance or even need replacement from time to time. Something that costs you money. God doesn't want you to try and recreate Him from your limited mind, utilizing limited resources and ultimately conform to that image yourself. The result would be death as with any religious approach to attain Godliness.

The Father holds you in the same esteem as His dear Son Jesus Christ. God sent His son to not only clear His name but to show us who we really are in Him. The Father sent the Son to restore His image to us so that we could be transformed to that perfect image and shed the old image.

God in our image

Man was deprived of the God that created everything good. God did not change, man did. Paul says we were enemies in our minds. Stuck in this rut we felt obliged to perform even more and this led to only more evil. Not only did knowing good and evil transform us into its likeness but it simultaneously made us the creators of our own reality. If we behaved good we received good, if we behaved bad we received bad. The better we performed, the better the reward would be. This became so bad that we started to create God in our own image. If were are vengeful towards our enemies, he would step up and be the reference for our vengeance. If you treated others on the basis of merit, so would your God, which is in fact in direct contrast with the Father who was in Christ reconciling the world to Himself not imputing their trespasses against them! If we only repaid someone for the good done toward us, so would he. If we loved only our own, he would also only love (us) his own. You see there are ample scripture in the bible to justify just about any God you want, but sadly most of them wouldn't get past Jesus. He is the only right interpretation of scripture and the only exegesis of the Father.

We live in a world which is unfortunately subject to the system of the tree of knowledge of good and evil and how this operates are evident in our daily lives. This contributes to the ease of falling into the snare of performance yet again. I mean, take the medical aid fund, my wife and I contribute toward on a monthly basis. To earn points, which are later converted to rewards and bonuses, you wear a wristband which monitors your heart-rate, counts your steps and shows how many calories you've burnt. All of these factors are then fed into your pc and you get points for each day's activity. Some car insurance companies install a device in your car that monitors your acceleration, general driving and speed and that is also converted into rewards, like receiving a percentage of your fuel expenses back in cash each month. We get caught up in a reward oriented way of life and without thinking we translate this way of life to the spirit and expect God to comply to a system that is not His heart. Now I am not saying you shouldn't take advantage of the benefits of the motor insurance deal when you are fit for it or to veer away from the fitness deal with the wristband if you are a natural when it comes to fitness and running around like a jack-rabbit. Take all the advantage you can, in moderation. What I am saying is that you shouldn't let this world with its reward oriented outlook dictate your relationships, friendships and ultimately, how you relate to God. This world will cause you to create God according to its image. You can participate in both of the above mentioned activities from a son position, without it having a voice concerning your identity.

What Would Jesus Do? – I thank God on a regular basis that the WWJD wristband and bumper-sticker frenzy blew over. What Would Jesus Do meant that God's ability was now at the mercy of our limited human ability. Here's what we did. Rather than consulting with Jesus on what He would do, by surveying His actions toward man in the gospels, we would hone in on our own ability in the concerned instance, utilizing our limited resources, and then proceed to do exactly the opposite to what He would do. Our behavior would be based on our deprived minds. Usually an eye for an eye, was applicable when someone wronged us. If you could forgive someone that has wronged you, then so could your god. If you were unable to show compassion to your enemies, guess what? Your god would follow suit. What Would Jesus Do was everything but Christocentric, as will-power and a conjured-up inner strength was the governing factor on what Jesus would have done at any given moment in our subjective experience. In other words – Jesus would be limited by our feeble human abilities, which is pretty lame.

Here's why grace is crucial in the interpretation of scripture. Grace is the Author. What better interpreter, than to sit down with the Author and have Him interpret the scriptures for you. Disregarding grace as hermeneutic approach in interpreting scriptures is the same as telling the Author He's not qualified to exegete His own work. The proper understanding of grace leads to proper exegesis of the scriptures.

Historical contextual hermeneutics is not a bad thing. On the contrary. It serves as a tool to determine the context in which things were perceived, as the composite title suggests. Yet this way of interpretation remains subject to the human experience at any given point in history. *"A carnal-man translation of a God (spiritual) thing"* comes to mind as we have seen earlier with unmerited favor as a failed attempt to define grace. Let us take the covenants as an example. God's character, nature and true intent with man was unknown, yet some individuals had been given a glimpse of His glory on occasion. If we want to apply historical contextual hermeneutics in interpreting the Father we also need to take the covenants into consideration, which in my opinion, and I'm speaking of the Mosaic covenant, is in direct conflict with His heart towards man. The Mosaic covenant was the understanding man had about God at that time, even though that was not God's ultimate, that was what they wanted.

Taking all these factors into consideration in trying to interpret God, we would be faced with a God we would want to embrace the one moment and commit to a nut-house the next. Our theology would be a mess featuring a Father that looks nothing like the Son, and our eschatology would be something along the lines of – *Jesus the machine-gun preacher and His Roman assassin side-kicks,* starring in the critically acclaimed blockbuster called: *70 A.D.*

Design

transitive verb
: to create, fashion, execute, or construct according to plan
: to devise for a specific function or end <*a book designed primarily as a college textbook*>

Image can also be seen as our divine design. We are designed to carry His burden and bare His yoke. One day I was driving to one of my plumbing suppliers for material and I got a whiff of burning rubber. I knew it wasn't my pick-up smelling like that, but checked the hood and in the mirrors to determine where the smell came from. I was ready to pull over just to be sure, when I looked up and saw another pick-up, 2 cars ahead of me, with black smoke whirling from both the back wheel arches. The excessive load on this vehicle was causing the body and the tires to rub on one another causing friction and resulting in the putrid burnt rubber smell. That pick up was designed to carry about 750 kg, but the load it was carrying exceeding that limit. That poor pick-up truck was performing a task that it wasn't designed for. And the sad thing is carrying that load would just result in death. Let's make it a bit more practical. An architect designs a bridge over a river for a purpose. You won't find an architect just designing a bridge willy nilly. No. He goes to the concerned area where the bridge is needed, determines what kind of traffic it would need to sustain, he considers the forces of nature and the risk of damage and more. Considering all of these in a worst case scenario, he then designs the bridge to fulfill all of these requirements. In this same way God creates man in His image for a purpose. His plan was to have beings on earth that contain His very life. For that He needed to create a vehicle that could contain this life or identity of His. What an amazing thought. We have for so long neglected our physical bodies and paid more attention to things we regard as more spiritual, while God's plan is to give immortality that very flesh of yours.

He needs your body to be able to influence others with His goodness. I mean, you've never heard of dead people doing evangelism! This reminds me of a joke. This young man inherits his grandfather's farm. Arriving there and having never seen this farm, he sets out on foot to do a bit of exploration of his own. Not taking into account on how early the sun sets in that part of the country, it is almost dark when he heads back. Suddenly his grandfather's ghost appears at the side of the road and as any ghost fearing young man, he starts running in the direction of the house. The ghost staying right beside him said: *"Son I want to tell you something!"* The young man replied: *"Granddad, if you don't mind, you can tell me while I'm running!"* Now imagine having to listen to a dead evangelist!

All jokes aside. Our physical bodies are important to God. If Jesus did not have a human body He would never have been able to influence us with the Father's love and we would still be oblivious of our His original intent. Jesus had to have a physical body to be the light of the world. When Jesus speaks to ordinary people and tells them about their heavenly

Father, He is not implying they are saved, but He is rather referring to their design. He is referring to the Father in whose image they were made. Man is made in God's image. We are His kind. He sees our state and knows we were made for His life. He makes an effort with us because He knows our potential.

Everyone has missed it as pertaining to relating to God in the proper way because they had the wrong impression about God's opinion about them. God designs man for His life. In other words. God creates man in His **image** for the purpose of His **likeness**. You and I were created to contain His life. His likeness. God wants man to choose His life, to become in His likeness from his own free-will.

Being created in God's image as our design has so many facets to it but one of the most important is that we have the capacity to become what we behold and believe. God speaks an unmistakable, universally understood, body language with us. God became man.... now meditate on that!

Adam and free-will

Every so often someone expresses their horror on social media following some terror attack, mass-shooting, national security threat or the Westboro Baptists disturbing the peace at a LGBTQ wedding or funeral. The odd and occasional reply to this post by someone possessing the same temperament leads as follows: *"Why can't people just love one another?"* The reason for this is simple: People don't know the concept of love and thus they are unable to dispense of it. Love has to be felt first, to get your head around it, so to speak. If all the new-agers and free-willers went on a *"loving everyone right"* rampage, not much would change because it doesn't fit our human design. Our design recognizes His love and reciprocates it effortlessly.

The concept of free-will has been pulled out of proportion by self-proclaimed free-thinkers to such an extent that some believe free-will can get them out of any situation. On the contrary, free-will has to be exercised toward something of substance, otherwise it is useless. Adam had exercised his free-will towards the wrong substance/system which got him into trouble. If free-will is the ultimate as it is claimed to be in some circles, then Adam could have *"free-willed"* himself out of that situation back into the garden. So yes, free-will is crucial but it is not the ultimate. Free-will has to be exercised toward substance. In our case, we are to place our faith in Jesus. If the old covenant law is your reference to godliness then your free-will only takes you back to square one. A futile exercise, but when exercised towards substance namely, the finished work of Jesus occupying a human body fully identifying with you, it's a whole different story with a surprisingly different outcome - His quality of life!

Divine design can be described as God believing in you. Because you are designed for something He knows you have the capacity for. You are designed for His identity, for Christ, His dear Son to live inside you. He is waiting in anticipation for your participation, for you to also believe it.

The serpent tells the woman that they were designed for something other than the life of God resulting in separation in their mind and the outcome being death. Free-will in choosing the wrong the wrong substance caused the fall of man and yet no amount of free-will exercising would change their fate. God had to intervene, eliminate the old man and supply the right substance (the finished work) man could exercise his faith toward.God placing you in Christ is not a violation of your free will. Before the incarnation of Jesus in human flesh, you had nothing to exercise your free will towards. God placing you in Christ is an empowerment handed to you to utilize your free-will!

Prior to the death and resurrection of Jesus, nobody could say: *"Hey guys, I'm fed up with this body of sin. I think I'll be a new creation!"* The reason being that nobody had any reference to anything better. They could not free-will themselves out of Adam. Also, God is not forcing Himself on anyone, not forcing anyone to partake. To be placed in Christ does not mean you are being forced to partake. You are restored to a platform of no condemnation, a clean slate, from which you can exercise your freedom of choice, to believe or not. You still have a choice. God *"places"* you in Christ as a gesture to show you that you belong. To be counted as lost you had to belong to begin with!

Male and female created He them

The good news of the gospel was imprinted into our design when God created man. By having Adam name the animals God wanted him to see for himself that among all of the creatures there was no-one his equal. This is just me. The way you would determine whether another creature of God is your equal is by procreating. I can already picture a certain critic of mine spreading on social media that I'm saying Adam had sex with all of the animals in his quest to find a mate. No. Laughs! However, what I am saying is that any form of racism is out the door if you apply just that. If you can procreate, you are equals. You and any other human from any other race can procreate. This also applies to us and God. Being created in His image means you have the capacity to possess everything He possesses. You and God are equals.

You can bear God's fruit. You were made for God's seed. You are His kind. God wanted Adam to see that he proceeded from Him, and the only way God could show him this, was by creating his mate (the woman) by taking her out of his own body. In the same way Adam in the image of God came out of God. God wanted to express His love to Adam in a tangible way. God gives man a woman and thus puts man in a position to understand His feelings towards him first hand. I always find it amusing as I notice some old school friends who never wanted anything to do with God and never paid much attention to christian student organizations, as they suddenly change their point of view when they start having children. It's like they have come to the end of themselves looking at their new born child, knowing that they couldn't do it out of themselves and then come to a sudden realization of how God feels about them when they are placed in the position of being a parent. It just shows that religion cannot show us our original design. Only God can do that. I am by no means saying that you won't experience God's love unless you have children. My wife and I don't have children but He has His ways to communicate to each and every one of us. God knows exactly how to speak to us. He made us. He knows our frame. He designed us and knows us inside-out.

When I read about the meaning of the word rib, as in the rib that God took from Adam's flesh, I cannot but think of a rib or plank of a barrel. The original Hebrew also refer to a plank. If you take one plank or rib out of a barrel it would not be able to hold any substance. It would be useless. I am not saying that you have to find someone to marry asap, otherwise you'll never be whole. No. If that was true only married couples would truly portray the image of God which is clearly not the case. Both man and woman was created in

His image. God knows exactly how to approach us. He makes necessary things relatable to broaden our understanding. God knows Adam inside out and knows exactly how to approach him. He designed him after all. Eve does not complete Adams image make-up. It just shows us that without Eve, Adam is lonely and longing. Like God is longing for us and want our fellowship from free-will. We proceeded from Him, remember? He longs for us. We are His removed rib.

"21 And the LORD God caused a deep sleep to fall upon Adam, and he slept: and he took one of his ribs, and closed up the flesh instead thereof; 22 And the rib, which the LORD God had taken from man, made he a woman, and brought her unto the man. 23 And Adam said, This is now bone of my bones, and flesh of my flesh: she shall be called Woman, because she was taken out of Man. 24 Therefore shall a man leave his father and his mother, and shall cleave unto his wife: and they shall be one flesh. 25 And they were both naked, the man and his wife, and were not ashamed."
Genesis 2:21-25 KJV

We need to consider something about Adam before we interpret this piece of scripture. Adam is a type of Him that was to come. Romans 5:14 says that everyone suffered death even them that did not sin after the similitude of Adam's transgression, who is the figure of Him that was to come. Him that was to come points to Jesus. So what was Jesus' transgression? 1 Tim 2:14 says that Adam was not deceived but the woman was deceived. Adam made a free-will decision to sin and go after Eve. He loved her so much that he gave up his innocence so he could be with her. Otherwise they would be separated. She would be evicted from the garden and he would remain there. In the same way Jesus went in after us and became sin for us, yet without sin. That was His *"transgression!"* A good transgression I might add. Jesus couldn't stand the thought of being without us. His unfailing love for us was the reason He left the awesome fellowship of the Trinity to take on our likeness so he could be with us. God loves us so much that He gave His word concerning us to take on our likeness in order for us to have access to His likeness. Jesus coming after us means we were taken out of Him. As we read Genesis 1:23-24 it shows how Adam was overwhelmed by the sight of Eve he uttered the following: " ....*A man shall leave his father and mother and cleave unto His wife and they shall be one flesh."* This Adamic prophecy not only shows our human design, but also what is reality in the spirit – how the Trinity operates. When fallen man is presented with his original design, the embedded, imprinted word concerning him or her makes it easy to relate back to his heavenly Father.

Now with the type and shadow in place we can properly dissect this piece of scripture. Adam fell into a deep sleep. This signifies Jesus' death. His death was our death. If one died all died. While He was *"sleeping"* we were taken out of Him. This is where the new creation man Paul talks about was born. I cannot find a better description for Paul's new creation people than just that. We were taken from Him in His *"sleep"*. Fallen man was transformed into a new creation by the death of Christ. You were taken out of Jesus. That makes you everything He is. If He is holy, so are you. If He is righteous, so are you! Are everyone aware of this? Like I said - that is why we call it evangelism! This is the good news of the gospel, right here in the book of Genesis!

CHAPTER 7
AFTER HIS LIKENESS

A*fter His likeness* was omitted from Genesis 1:27 with reason. The reason is simple. His likeness is immortality or to have eternal life. Now for those who realize God as love, this makes perfect sense. He wants to grant immortality to people acknowledging they were made in His image, people who recognize their design and acquired the accompanying identity. Let's say someone is still stuck in a religious rut of inferiority complex in regards to the Father. God is just and righteous not to grant such a person immortality with good reason.

The reason being that the person would enter eternity feeling inferior, not able to receive anything from God. This person would not be of the same mind as God. This here might be hard to swallow but if we take a look at the eviction of mankind from the garden – it is exactly that. This also shows how much we need God's long suffering. He is not willing that any should perish, but that they may come to the truth. Immortality, or more fitting, to be created after His likeness is the inheritance of the saints. *"Yes Jan, but you implied earlier that all were made saints. Aren't you contradicting yourself?"*

No. The difference is whether or not you know or acknowledge that you're a saint. Adam, or rather the woman, forfeited exactly this and fell short of being created after God's likeness. Jesus gave up on His immortality (the God likeness) and took on our likeness (mortality) to redeem us from a false design system and then subsequently instate His likeness to us. When we comply we shall be like Him. We would be created after His likeness (immortal.)

*"2 Beloved, now are we the sons of God, and it doth not yet appear what we shall be: but we know that, when he shall appear, we shall be **like** him; for we shall see him as he is. 3 And every man that hath this hope in him purifieth himself, even as he is pure."* 1 John 3:2-3 KJV

"2 But friends, that's exactly who we are: children of God. And that's only the beginning. Who knows how we'll end up! What we know is that when Christ is openly revealed, we'll see him—and in seeing him, become like him. 3 All of us who look forward to his Coming stay ready, with the glistening purity of Jesus' life as a model for our own."
1 John 3:2-3 The Message

Here the Apostle John states that we are already the sons of God, yet we have nothing to prove it in the physical. We don't know what we will look like, all we know is we will look like Jesus. We are still stuck in a human body which is subject to decay. Note that our bodies are not evil and we are not in dire need to be redeemed from it. Our bodies are subject to physical death. In this same way our mind and spirit were subject to a wrong belief system without hope.

"To whom God would make known what is the riches of the glory of this mystery among the Gentiles; which is Christ in you, the hope of glory:" Colossians 1:27 KJV

Before the Father raised Jesus from the dead, no-one possessed immortality. Yes, people were physically raised from the dead but they were still subject to physical death and these occurrences are not to be confused with immortality. Immortality was the mystery of the ages. Even in modern day movies we see man's endless conquest to find an elixir to obtain eternal life. Unfortunately these attempts are futile because the point of departure is rooted in the wisdom of the serpent.

Many a church or *"movement"* make it their mission to manifest the sons of God, but fail to recognize the context Paul was trying to convey. Do you see the danger of reading Paul's grace oriented writings through the eyes of the law? Applying the wisdom of the serpent in order to get God to move or manifest something? Let me assure you. Nothing you **do** will convince God to give you immortality. It is what y o u **believe** that will grant you to be created after His likeness - for you to obtain immortality.

Christ in you is the condition. God gives immortality to Christ-likeness. Christ in the believer is the seal for our hope. *".... the hope of glory"* in Colossians1:27 is also translated: The hope of the manifestation of the sons. So if you want people to be manifested sons, preach the gospel in order for them to get Christ in them.

Here's another condition.

*"He that hath an ear, let him hear what the Spirit saith unto the churches; To him that **overcometh** will I give to eat of the **tree of life**, which is in the midst of the paradise of God."*
Revelation 2:7 KJV

Note: *"he who overcomes."* This is the person who stands on the finished work. He/she places their faith in that which was already accomplished on their behalf. God does not want any to perish according to John 3:16, but that they would have eternal life. He wants to give man eternal life but He wants man's mind to be in order before He does that. He is long-suffering so people can come to the right view of Him and themselves. He wants to energize the right *confession* or *conviction* if you will, onto immortality. God wants your confession of your self to coincide with His confession of you.

In this same manner He wanted His glory on the earth. His glory to reign over all he has made. To contain this glory and life He first had to create a vehicle with the capacity to contain it. That vehicle is man. Man created in His image. Likeness in Hebrew refers to resemblance or a concrete model meaning that if man was to partake of God's life in God's way he would be a complete resemblance or concrete model of the Godhead.

As we've already noticed, the likeness part was omitted in Genesis 1:27. Now the only two verses that vaguely refer to anything similar to likeness we find in the conversation between the Woman and the serpent and after the eviction of man from the garden. The serpent says the following:

First instance:

*"For God doth know that in the day ye eat thereof, then your eyes shall be opened, and ye shall be **as gods**, knowing good and evil."* Genesis 3:5 KJV

The wisdom of the serpent is anything outside of the gospel that promises eternal life or immortality. Jesus would later confront the seed of the serpent with the following:

"Search the scriptures; for in them ye think ye have eternal life: and they are they which testify of me."
John 5:39 KJV

The scriptures they were searching was the law. Here Jesus shows them the futility of chasing after eternal life in applying the wisdom of the serpent. We obtain this *"wisdom"* by partaking of the tree of knowledge of good and evil. By adhering to this message you are forcing a different load with different specifications on God's design. In doing this a load is placed on man that he wasn't designed for. God says that if they ate from that tree they would surely die. This in the original language is likened unto a death sentence. One translation reads as follows: *"Of this death, you shall die."* - meaning that this system will ruin your quality of life in the here and now and it will ultimately reward you with death.

You would be subject to disease (wisdom of the serpent) that would ultimately kill you. More light is shed on this when I discuss the tree of knowledge of good and evil. Someone on death row has anything but a fun time awaiting their execution. So while he is waiting everything he does is meaningless and fruitless. The outcome is death. The serpent told the woman that in partaking from the tree of knowledge of good and evil they would become as gods and so attain to God's likeness.

The **second instance** where we note something similar to the likeness of God is in Genesis 3:22 after partaking of the tree of knowledge of good and evil.

*"And the LORD God said, Behold, the man is become **as one of us**, to know good and evil: and now, lest he put forth his hand, and take also of the tree of life, and eat, and live for ever:"*
Genesis 3:22 KJV

Man chose the wisdom of the serpent as a means to obtain eternal life. If you would allow me, I would translate Genesis 3:22 to something along the lines of: *"Man chose to work his way towards Our quality of life (within the confines of time/mortality) in an attempt to obtain eternal life by his own effort."*

Now some would argue that God finds His being in the experiential knowledge of good and evil, by implying that the tree of knowledge of good and evil was there only for His enjoyment. My question is this: *"If I'm created in His image, with the capacity to contain everything He already possesses, why then would He keep anything from me?"* The answer is simple: *"You will die if you eat of it"* You what? He doesn't want that! He wants you to live your full potential in Him. He entertains good thoughts of life for you!

".... thou shalt not eat of it: for in the day that thou eatest thereof thou shalt surely die."
Genesis 2:17 KJV

In saying that it's God's tree, you are implying that God is the author of death. This could not be further from the truth. In fact, the mere existence of this tree really emphasizes the fact that God provides freedom of choice to His creation. We have a choice to how we wish to relate to Him and this is exactly what Genesis 3:22 implies.

God does not possess experiential knowledge of good and evil. He possesses experiential knowledge of faith in the dynamics of the Trinity.

We will look into the meaning of knowing good and evil in a while. Meanwhile we see there are two ways to obtain His likeness and only one delivers on its promise.

Obtaining His likeness by recognizing and agreeing with

our original design (the risen Jesus) or partaking from the tree of knowledge of good and evil. The one energizes your innocence onto eternal life and the other results in you losing your innocence and the outcome is death. Life on death row.

CHAPTER 8
ENCULTURATION

"Look man, I lay it out for y'all to play it out."
- Huggy Bear (Starsky & Hutch)

Many view of the garden is God laying it out in the natural, for mankind to play it out and get enculturated or influenced to who He is and who they are. To see the unseen as we get to know Him. In this process, God is showing man His objective, mans' original design. He then leaves it up to man to do his own exploration and discovery.

Enculturation is defined as the process by which an individual learns the traditional content of a culture and assimilates its practices and values. When approached from a psychological angle it is defined as follows:

"A process starting in early childhood where cultural values, ideas etc are instilled into members of the society."

Enculturation in layman's terms, can be described as taking a baby from a clean slate and then influencing it with the life you, the parent, already possess. The influence of the parent on the child could be both positive and negative. The parent can project hopes and positivity to the child but also fears and feelings of inferiority. This child will then grow up mimicking his or her parents in their mannerisms and habits. We've all seen how the little ones suck up everything we say like sponges. You know, those cute moments when they pretend to be calling grandma on the cellphone or repeat a profanity you yelled at someone who cut you off in traffic. None of your actions, though you're not always aware of it yourself, goes unnoticed.

The only difference with God is that we don't acquire His Life by mimicking Him. That is the very thing the tree of knowledge of good and evil advocates. Behavior modification neither saves you, nor give you His quality of life. To say the least. It doesn't even bring God closer. God wants to touch our hearts with His goodness and by doing that, influence us for the good. He speaks to the very depths of our being. There is no person on the face of the earth that is not made in His image. Not a single one that does not possess the capacity to contain His very life in them. Such a person does not exist.

In my line of work I have access to all sorts of households and different scenarios. One of those are a family that opened their home to serve as a safe haven for mothers that wanted to give their babies up for adoption, as in some cases they could not take care of them or simply because they didn't want them. Sad thought I know. This family takes in as many babies as their home allows and provides formula, food and clothing out of their own pockets. The babies then remain there until they are adopted. The family took in a baby boy. They grew fond of him and decided to adopt him as their own. I have to add that the family is white and the majority of children that go through that safe haven are black or colored. This has nothing to do with race or racism for those who are concerned. If you can look past race this will greatly benefit you in understanding what I am trying to convey as pertaining to enculturation. This specific little boy, although he is black himself, is scared of black people. He sees his adoptive mom, a white woman, treating him as her equal, feeding him, defending him, changing his diapers as she would her own biological children. The influence this man and his wife has on him, in treating him in that manner, automatically makes him think that he is their equal and in simpler terms, he thinks he is white. This one day as I was working there, and that specific day they had quite an influx of babies and that required that them to get reinforcements.

So they hired a help, a black lady. This little boy cried and wanted nothing to do with her. The lady later told me that they would have to get that same help on a regular basis in order for the boy to get used to black people. This little boy's story touched me in a way that made me see the way God wants us to acquire His quality of life by us seeing ourselves as His equal. Equal to the extent that you get a fright when you look back at where you came from. I had this very experience the other day as I stumbled upon a video of the *"apostle"* we *"submitted"* to in ministry. Before he started preaching at this church all sorts of devils were shouted at and the strong man was bound. At first I was quite amused because I haven't seen that sort of action since I've been in grace. I was ready to get the pop corn out! Even Jezebel was rebuked, kicked around and later bound so she couldn't manipulate anyone. When they then deemed the air *"clean"* the sermon was delivered and my utter amusement turned to sadness as I looked upon people that still don't know the immense love our Father has for them. This video ultimately scared me, scared me to the fact that it could have been me and as a matter of fact, a decade or longer ago, had been me. What I am today is only by His grace. I really cannot boast in myself because I know my efforts would have gone pear-shaped. My works could never give me the life I now possess in God. My works would definitely have made it worse, way worse!

Another example of enculturation, or rather the lack thereof, is in the case of feral children. There are countless accounts of children who were abandoned in the wild or somehow just went missing. Subsequently these children were then adopted into a family of monkeys or wolves or even got by on their own in the wild to the surprise of many. In all feral children cases the verdict was the same. After coming into contact with civilization following their rescue, they would lack enculturation. They would lack the ability to talk, eating habits would be animal-like, and social skills would vary within the parameters of both extremes. Just as in the case of feral children, we were indoctrinated by a system that promoted a warped perspective of the Father, that caused us to conform to its design.

In the case of the first people, Adam and the woman, God placed them in the garden to play it out as I would like to call it, and be exposed to His enculturation/influence from a clean slate. By them acquiring their identity, whether good or bad, caused them to mature. This is evident when we consider that they only procreated after choosing religion, or rather failing to acquire their source of life by recognizing their design.

Scientists found that baby birds that learn the song of their particular species, already have the song in them and when they hear it, they *"learn"* it. They learn the song that was inside them all along. They just need a nudge from someone that looks exactly like them to show them what is already theirs, what is already at their disposal. This makes me think that it is exactly the concept God had in mind when He created man.

Eat from all the trees in the garden

God uses natural things to convey truths in order for us to understand spiritual things. Jesus told stories also known as parables to His disciples and crowds that would listen to Him, to make spiritual things more relatable. He understood the cultural and social scene and used every day examples to get the truth across.

Now in the same way God uses the analogy of trees to convey something of significance in the garden. The same way a baby and progressively a young child gets influenced by their surroundings by which they form their identity, was also the intention of our Father with man in the garden of His delight. God in His wisdom made provision for this when He told man to eat from all the trees of the garden. There were two trees in the middle of the garden yes. But that doesn't mean these two trees were the only trees. These "other" trees were placed there to bring man to maturity from his infant spiritual state. These are the trees of righteousness as noted in Isaiah 61:3

".......that they might be called trees of righteousness, the planting of the Lord, that He might be glorified."

A tree of righteousness is the Lord's planting. They are the Lord's doing and they won't hesitate to tell you just that.

Their righteousness is not their own. These trees testify of their Creator's righteousness. His righteous dealing with them. They are the result of His righteousness. The fruit they bear are not their own. They are planted by the waters and they ascribe the nourishment and fruit they bear all back to Him. These trees have no care in the world because they are planted by the waters. So when God tells man to eat from all these other trees, He wants man to be influenced by their testimony.

"7 Blessed is the man that trusteth in the LORD, and whose hope the LORD is. 8 For he shall be as a tree planted by the waters, and that spreadeth out her roots by the river, and shall not see when heat cometh, but her leaf shall be green; and shall not be careful in the year of drought, neither shall cease from yielding fruit." Jeremiah 17:7-8 KJV

Now these trees were placed in the garden with a purpose. Isaiah 61 refers to them as trees of righteousness, the planting of the Lord, to Glorify Him. If you and I were to encounter these trees, their response would most likely be something along the lines of:

"Everything I am is because of God. He planted me. He sustains me. The fruit I bear is His, I just bear it. I am a result of His righteousness – Him doing the right thing to His creation."

Remember Adam and Eve was only innocent and was yet to have the life of God in them. Man had ample resources in the garden concerning God's goodness in order for him to make an informed decision. The other trees were placed there so Adam could taste and see that God is good. So he could see what a person would look like that partook of God's life, meaning someone agreeing with God's opinion about them.

As we know Adam was only a living soul and his *"job"* was to only agree with what God already said about him. This would also be the means by which the woman would have overcome the snare of the serpent.

God telling them to partake from all the trees was symbolic of God providing the right school and surroundings of enculturation, for them to mature in, by discovering their design and acquiring their identity in Him.

CHAPTER 9
THE TREE OF KNOWLEDGE
OF GOOD AND EVIL

With man's free-will in mind, God allowed the existence of another tree. The tree of knowledge of good and evil. A tree planted by Him. A tree that was created good, but turned bad on its own account. God creates everything good but leaves it with its own freedom of choice. This tree was allowed to remain in the garden for man to exercise his free-will.

God gives you all the reason to stay but He won't keep you there against your will. What honor do you have in creating robots that sing your praises in the absence of free-will? That would be a joke right? But if your creation sang your praises because they really wanted to, because they cannot contain themselves at the very thought of your goodness and your righteous acts towards them. Then my friend, you deserve all the honor and praise that's coming your way. This is the good God I'm talking about. He has integrity and stays true to His character throughout the whole bible. He is only good. He only creates good.

Now as we've seen this tree turned bad and God forbade eating from it. This tree ascribed all of God's good attributes and nourishment it received from Him to itself.

"7 Thus was he fair in his greatness, in the length of his branches: for his root was by great waters. 8 The cedars in the garden of God could not hide him: the fir trees were not like his boughs, and the chestnut trees were not like his branches; nor any tree in the garden of God was like unto him in his beauty. 9 I have made him fair by the multitude of his branches: so that all the trees of Eden, that were in the garden of God, envied him."
Ezekiel 31:7-9 KJV

First of all, eating of this tree is not stealing or eating the tithe. God help us! Many a charlatan and wolf in sheep's clothing have been fleecing God's people with this sort of utter nonsense. That is just messed up. The tree of knowledge of good and evil was never God's tree or His portion forbidden to man. Laughs! The law of forbidden things, imagine that! If you are saying that this tree, the tree of knowledge of good and evil, is God's tree and only there for His use and enjoyment, you are actually saying that God has to work to maintain His identity, which is utter nonsense. God does not need to perform to be. He just is! The Trinity functions in a mutual fellowship of believing in one another. If you are looking for proper teaching on tithing though, you can read: *Jesus is the Tithe*, written by my friend and mentor Bertie Brits. I had the privilege to read the electronic version before it was sent to the printers and as you are reading this it would already be available. The tree of knowledge of good and evil is summed up in short as: The *"system"* by which you aspire to be like God by your own effort. This is also what we know the law does. Even though the law was only written down much later, nonetheless this was the birthplace of that system. Another way to relate to God and sadly never achieving it. A never ending cycle. Good is translated – God, as in there is no one good except God. Good and God are synonymous in the ancient world.Evil is translated – **full of labors** in Greek – **distress and sorrow** in Hebrew. Does that sound like God's tree? Is God full of labors, in distress and sorrow? Laughs! No God is at rest. He has been at rest all along.

Jesus says:

"Come unto me, all ye that labor and are heavy laden, and I will give you rest." Matthew 11:28 KJV

Jesus invites all that have partaken of this tree (**all ye that labor**) in an attempt to relate to God to come to Him so He can give them rest.

God's definition of evil is this: You, His child, someone created to resemble Him, having to **work to obtain** His life instead of receiving it free of charge! Not you as a person – the working to obtain part. The tree of knowledge of good and evil can't possibly be God's tree. It's in direct contrast with His character.

On a different approach to the meaning, the term *"good and evil"* is a figure of speech known as a merism, connecting words with the opposite meaning to create one general expression. An old Egyptian expression *"evil-good"* would simply imply *"everything"* meaning God and everything outside of God, wrapped up in one word. One meaning. One identity. Almost like the yin-yang in eastern mythology. You cannot separate God from your effort and sorrowful labor. All the good you will experience in life would be accompanied by your labor, your effort, your sorrow. (God) good things, like blessings would be inseparably accompanied by your works or having to give up on something you really treasured. You cannot have the one without the other. Someone would do something good for you and instinctively you would be on the look-out for the evil twin to make its appearance and take its due.

When God said that man had become *"as one of Us"* by knowing good and evil it wasn't a good thing. What He actually meant was that man chose to relate to Him on the basis of his performance. Partaking from this tree in the form of its fruit caused man to adhere to its flawed word or message concerning God. If eaten, a misrepresentation of who God is would be your portion. All the good in this life would be ascribed to God but sadly also all the bad that happens to us would also be ascribed to Him. A complete mess. A mess only He could save us from. When Jesus arrives on the scene, the bible says, He came to His own and His own knew Him not. The law and religious system was so corrupted by the theology of the serpent that when God got on the scene, He was treated as a stranger.

Burnt out

Have you ever come across someone so burnt out on religion that they want nothing to do with God that they can't stand the mention of His name in a conversation? I was there, I know exactly what that feels like. I was working in England then, and some of my family members and friends also worked and lived in London. One day after my departure from christianity someone mentioned a *"new"* church they had discovered, and I made no secret of my feelings about christianity and God. I was worn out and was left feeling inadequate of ever attaining any good standing with God. So I thought, screw this. I don't care anymore. *"If you're there God, good on you, but I just can't do this anymore!"* I was oblivious to His love for me and could not see Him being good and only good. Him being good was always accompanied by my effort and to say the least I couldn't make myself do that anymore. If His goodness depended on me and my behavior, then He probably wasn't worth my while in the first place. Like with my case and others, we could not see Him for who He is and in turn we couldn't see ourselves as He sees us. This causes more problems and one of those is a identity crisis. Thank you Jesus for setting things straight again. Don't you just love Him for loving us so much? He loved us so much that He could not stay in the Father's house without us! Like Adam, a type of Jesus said:

"Therefore shall a man leave his father and his mother, and shall cleave unto his wife: and they shall be one flesh."
Genesis 2:26 KJV

Jesus couldn't stand the fact of being without us. He came in after us, taking on our likeness to redeem us from the system of the tree of knowledge of good and evil. We are His woman!

"Are you tired? Worn out? Burned out on religion? Come to me. Get away with me and you'll recover your life. I'll show you how to take a real rest. Walk with me and work with me—watch how I do it. Learn the unforced rhythms of grace. I won't lay anything heavy or ill-fitting on you. Keep company with me and you'll learn to live freely and lightly."
Matthew 11:28-30 The Message

Does this in any way sound like someone that wants to

take advantage of you or do you any harm? No, this is our lovely Lord who wants to serve you with His life!

The serpent and his seed

"Now the serpent was more subtil than any beast of the field which the LORD God had made. And he said unto the woman, Yea, hath God said, Ye shall not eat of every tree of the garden?" Genesis 3:1 KJV
Some facts on the serpent:

1. The serpent was a created being. Initially created by God just like all other creatures were created good. God's initial purpose with the serpent is unclear but considering the fact that it was created good, God probably had a better purpose with it in serving mankind rather than spreading lies about Him.

2. The serpent "was" more subtle than any beast of the field....
   "Was" is translated **"hâyâh"**which means **"had become"** in the original Hebrew. This has the same meaning as the **was** we find in Genesis 1:2. "And the earth **was/"hâyâh"/had become So the serpent was created good but became more subtle than the other beasts.**
   Maybe his ability to speak formed part of him **becoming** more subtle than the other beasts of the field.
   "14 And no marvel; for Satan himself is transformed into an angel of light. 15 Therefore it is no great thing if his ministers also be transformed as the ministers of righteousness; whose end shall be according to their works." 2 Corinthians 11:14-15 KJV

3. Considering the above scripture there is no doubt in my mind that the serpent could take on the form of those whom he wanted to deceive in order to influence them. He was the evangelist or advocate of the tree of knowledge of good and evil remember? Deception comes all dressed up – looking like the real thing, hence Paul's expression - *"angel of light."* He also tells the church in Galatia to remain in the message he first brought them, and warns not to heed any other, not even if an angel descended from heaven brought another gospel. (Galatians 1:8)
    2 Corinthians 11:15 " *Therefore it is no great thing if **his ministers** also be **transformed** as the ministers of righteousness....* "

4. The serpent was a resident in the garden. He knew what God had commanded man concerning the eating from the trees and the order to abstain from eating from the tree of knowledge of good and evil. So why would God place a serpent with malicious intentions in the garden and to top that, place the tree of knowledge of good and evil in the middle of the garden? A tree that is the exact opposite of His nature? The answer is simple. Freedom. Freedom to choose. God is not a control freak and if you're going to be devoted to Him, He wants you to do that from a platform of freedom.

So what about the serpent's seed? Does the serpent have physical offspring roaming the earth today? Heavens no! God help us! If you thought I was going to add fuel to your fire concerning giants and the Nephilim, then I am sorry to disappoint you.

Allow me to explain the serpent's seed.

"Ye are of your father the devil, and the lusts of your father ye will do. He was a murderer from the beginning, and abode not in the truth, because there is no truth in him. When he speaketh a lie, he speaketh of his own: for he is a liar, and the father of it." John 8:44 KJV

Here Jesus is addressing human beings (the religious institution of the day) that bought into the lie of the devil. People that found their life in the wisdom of the serpent. In buying into this, they deemed it necessary to spread this wisdom of works righteousness they have obtained, to the rest of the world. The seed of the tree of knowledge of good and evil likes likeminded company and it wants to replicate as would any other seed. The principle remains the same.

"But the fearful, and unbelieving, and the abominable, and murderers, and whoremongers, and sorcerers, and idolaters, and all liars, shall have their part in the lake which burneth with fire and brimstone: which is the second death."
Revelation 21:8 KJV

Wait a minute! Did John just say that liars shall also have their part in the lake of fire? What if I failed to do my homework and told the teacher the dog ate it? That's a lie right? That makes me a liar right? RIGHT? Yes, but that sort of fib cannot be compared to unbelief, murder, whore-mongering, sorcery or idolatry. I am in no way condoning your dishonesty in lying to the teacher, but the liars John is addressing are quite different. The blatantly lie about God. Just like the serpent, the Pharisees and the scribes of Jesus' day lied about God. He is referring to them as the children of the father of lies. See John 8:44

"But when he saw many of the Pharisees and Sadducees come to his baptism, he said unto them, O generation of vipers, who hath warned you to flee from the wrath to come
Matthew 3:7 KJV

Here John the Baptist is addressing the pharisees and scribes, sent out to keep an eye on him as he baptized people with the baptism of repentance. He is not referring to them as physical offspring of the serpent but as people that bought into the lie of devil and thus have the devil as their father. They were subject to a system that brought about death in them through sin, hence – their father being the devil.

"34 O generation of vipers, how can ye, being evil, speak good things? for out of the abundance of the heart the mouth speaketh. 35 A good man out of the good treasure of the heart bringeth forth good things: and an evil man out of the evil treasure bringeth forth evil things."
Matthew 12:34-35 KJV

Here the principle, *"You cannot give out that which you do not already possess yourself"* is applicable. In this piece of scripture Jesus is addressing the *"seed"* of the serpent, set out to oppose Him. These are not the physical seed of the serpent and most certainly not the generation that would pay for all the bloodshed since the murder of Abel. He is addressing a belief system.

Jesus shows man his design, shows him that he is the pick-up truck (capacity/design-restored) by presenting him with the appropriate load for the truck (His identity/ LIFE), while the seed of the serpent, posing as God's agents, tries to convince man that he was created for a different (identity) load and by doing that makes them miss the ultimate destination – eternal life!

CHAPTER 10
OBJECTIVE & SUBJECTIVE
REALITIES

"One of the biggest stumbling blocks to understanding what the gospel message is and to finding the life of God being born in people is that we have confused the identity of man with the design of man. And we have made them as if they are one in the same." - Greg Henry

"Christ's objective (general) work is finished REGARDLESS of our response. To enjoy it, we respond subjectively (personally)." - John J. Withington

Understanding the dynamics of objective truth (God's view) and man's subjective participation (man's agreement with that truth) eliminates a lot of confusion in the area of innocence/ inclusion and salvation.

*"For **God so loved** the world, that he **gave** his only begotten Son, that **whosoever believeth** in him should **not perish**, but have **everlasting life**."* John 3:16 KJV

God so loved the world that He gave Jesus – whosoever believes should not perish but have eternal life. We see God's objective in this very well known scripture as pertaining to Him restoring access to the Tree of Life to mankind. Man could not partake from the Tree of Life whilst being an enemy in his mind. God sent Jesus to restore the image in which man was created and in doing that, restores man's right to the Tree of Life/immortality. God's ultimate for man is man having His quality of life in the here and now and when this life is acquired by man subjectively, that is agreeing with God's view, that very Life overflows into eternity. That agreement with God mindset or conviction then gets *"rewarded"* with immortality.

*"And that **he died for all**, that they which live **should not henceforth live unto themselves**, but unto him which died for them, and rose again."* 2 Corinthians 5:15 KJV

He died for all – you no longer have to live unto yourself. Your old self is in fact dead. Jesus died as you. You are now enabled to live unto Him. You now have substance to which you can exercise your faith through free will.

*"1 9 To wit, that God was in Christ, **reconciling the world unto himself**, not imputing their trespasses unto them; and hath committed unto us the word of reconciliation. 2 0 Now then we are ambassadors for Christ, as though God did beseech you by us: we pray you in Christ's stead, **be ye reconciled to God.**"*
2 Corinthians 5:19-20 KJV

God has reconciled the world to Himself – be reconciled to God. We established earlier as pertaining to the meaning of the word reconcile that God views man as His equal. With this in mind, it makes it easier to understand God's objective and the importance of us agreeing with that subjectively and sharing and enjoying the benefits that comes with that.

"1 Therefore being justified by faith, we have peace with God through our Lord Jesus Christ: 2 By whom also we have access by faith into this grace wherein we stand, and rejoice in hope of the glory of God."
Romans 5:1-2 KJV

We have already established in an earlier chapter, how righteousness and justification works. We are already justified, righteous, innocent and blameless, but faith in Jesus causes us to access it. You see, someone unaware of the fact that God is at peace with them would in return not experience peace with God. Faith frees up that peace. (Romans 5:1)

Now look at how verse two accentuates exactly that and even elaborates the dynamic of verse one. Verse two says we are already standing in grace. We are placed in Christ. This is **God's objective.** Note that this precedes faith and also puts faith in the right perspective. Faith is our access to tap into this grace. This grace becomes alive to us as we believe. This is **our subjective** participation to what He already believes about us. This gives us a brand new perspective in viewing righteousness. Greg Henry from Gospel Revolution Church - Slidell, Louisiana, has more proper teaching on this perspective in his teaching called: The Gift Of Righteousness.

I can already hear someone saying: *"But it's the faith OF Jesus that saved me!"* You know who you are. You hang in there - Paul will address that shortly.

CHAPTER 11
THE DYNAMICS OF HIS FAITH

"Disobedience to God is to refuse
to let your heart be persuaded by Him"
- Greg Henry.

Hearing God is an inevitable part of our design. Faith should be seen as a fruit of our design, which is the sole doing of God, instead of the means to bring about the doing of God. Romans 10:17 shows us the dynamics that brings about faith.

"So then faith cometh by hearing, and hearing by the word of God." Romans 10:17 KJV

This is a chain reaction. The word shows up, activates hearing and hearing activates faith. The Word comes onto the scene, revives design, that is, God's original intent with the individual and that in turn brings about faith. Hearing activates faith as you apply free-will. Simply put, Jesus steps into your darkness, shows you Gods' opinion of you (you included in the finished work) and you choose to believe or not to believe. Considering these dynamics, do you see how crucial it is to be sure you are busy with the Gospel and not scaring people off God with a different gospel? Now on addressing people's original design by preaching the good news does not mean everyone will turn, as some love darkness (their version of light) more, as seen in John 1.

"Hey, remember Me? I made you! This is what I believe about you! This is what you actually look like. This is what your Father looks like."

In this, hearing that forms part of our design, gets activated. Ever wondered why some don't heed the street preacher that spews condemnation? That is because we were created to react on the truth. No one gets filled with awe, love and passion on hearing they are rejected? That doesn't make sense. On the other hand, if this was how you were taught to perceive God, condemnation and guilt would win you back to that particular flock.

Saul of Tarsus, consumed by religious zeal, embarked on a trip to Damascus to persecute the very young church of Jesus Christ. En-route he had an encounter with Jesus that changed his life forever.

"3 And as he journeyed, he came near Damascus: and suddenly there shined round about him a light from heaven: 4 And he fell to the earth, and heard a voice saying unto him, Saul, Saul, why persecutest thou me? 5 And he said, Who art thou, Lord? And the Lord said, I am Jesus whom thou persecutest: it is hard for thee to kick against the pricks." Acts 9:3-5 KJV

Jesus had been speaking to Saul, aside from his lack of faith. Inside the package of our human design in His image is the ability to hear Him. This ability has absolutely no relation to our performance. If hearing Him was a result of good behavior or our self effort righteousness, I'm afraid we would be screwed proper.

In persecuting the church, Saul was kicking against God's design and that design was to accept Jesus. Jesus tells Paul that He is actually going against his design by denying people access to salvation in Jesus. *"You are persecuting Me!"* This also emphasizes freedom of choice and implies that you have the option to believe or not to believe the good news.

*"18 The Spirit of the Lord is upon me, because he hath anointed me to preach the gospel to the poor; he hath sent me to heal the brokenhearted, to preach deliverance to the captives, and recovering of sight to the blind, to set at liberty them that are bruised, 19 To preach the acceptable year of the Lord. 20 And he closed the book, and he gave it again to the minister, and sat down. And the eyes of all them that were in the synagogue were fastened on him. 21 And he began to say unto them, This day is this scripture fulfilled in your **ears**. 22 And all bare him witness, and wondered at the gracious words which proceeded out of his mouth. And they said, Is not this Joseph's son?"*
Luke 4:18-22 KJV

*"6 Sacrifice and offering thou didst not desire; mine **ears** hast thou opened: burnt offering and sin offering hast thou not required. 7 Then said I, Lo, I come: in the volume of the book it is written of me."*
Psalm 40:6-7 KJV

*"51 Ye stiffnecked and uncircumcised in heart and **ears**, ye do always resist the Holy Ghost: as your fathers did, so do ye. 52 Which of the prophets have not your fathers persecuted? and they have slain them which shewed before of the coming of the Just One; of whom ye have been now the betrayers and murderers: 53 Who have received the law by the disposition of angels, and have not kept it. 54 When they heard these things,*

*they were cut to the heart, and **they gnashed on him with their teeth**. 55 But he, being full of the Holy Ghost, looked up stedfastly into heaven, and saw the glory of God, and Jesus standing on the right hand of God,56 And said, Behold, I see the heavens opened, and **the Son of man standing on the right hand of God**. 57 Then they cried out with a loud voice, and **stopped their ears**, and ran upon him with one accord, 58 And cast him out of the city, and stoned him: and the witnesses laid down their clothes at a young man's feet, whose name was Saul."* Acts 7:51-58 KJV

Jesus says: *"My sheep hear my voice and they follow me."* Everyone has the ability to recognize the truth by their original design, but not everyone chooses to pursue it. This scripture is actually a telling of the testimony and demise of Stephen but we see a different side to it in these Pharisees rejecting God's objective not only towards them, but towards every human being. The guys who gnashed their teeth and stopped their ears, heard the truth about them, but they had too much invested in their god and his petty system. This is exactly what Paul was talking about regarding the suppression of the truth in unrighteousness as he addressed the Romans.

"18 For the wrath of God is revealed from heaven against all ungodliness and unrighteousness of men, who hold the truth in unrighteousness; 19 Because that which may be known of God is manifest in them; for God hath shewed it unto them."
Romans 1:18-19 KJV

On the bright side, the fullness of being created in the image of God comes to fulfillment in our subjective participation in connection with that design. The result of which is having his quality of life and being an heir of eternal life. God only has life in mind for you.

Faith is being treated like a cuss word in some *"grace"* circles. I believe in the inclusion of mankind in-Christ but I am also a faith proponent. These two are independent but functions at optimum level in harmony. In easier language it would be design and identity as earlier discussed. This is confusing to some, because they fail to listen to what you actually profess as they would rather dig into their limited religious frame of reference, to label you a false teacher. Tiresome, I tell you! Subjective participation is the distinguishing factor to prevent confusion, in my opinion. Some have an issue with faith and some claim it's not necessary. If you've already made up your mind as to what you think I believe. Hold that thought and hear me out as to what I believe concerning faith.

Here's my response to that statement saying: *"But it's the faith of Jesus that saved me!"* To tell you the truth – I couldn't agree more. Here's why: *He is the Author and the finisher of our faith, right? Right on!* That means He wrote the faith manual concerning relating with the Father. Remember, He did not believe subjectively on your behalf. That would rule out your freedom of choice.

His faith is the objective truth concerning you and I. So how does His faith save me. We are saved by utilizing His version or *"brand"* of faith when we see ourselves included in His very humanity. The power of identification was on display as He finished the work as us. In doing that He lets us in on the dynamics of faith in the Trinity. This is how His (brand of) faith saved us. Before His *"brand"* of faith we only had religion and law in our frame of reference regarding relating to the Father.

Let's see how Jesus achieved in setting up His brand of faith as the standard to which we have access to the Father.

*"8 Though he were a Son, yet learned he obedience by the things which he **suffered**; 9 And being made perfect, he became the author of eternal salvation unto all them that obey him;"*
Hebrews 5:8-9 KJV

"Though He were a Son ...." implies belonging and/or inclusion. He was a Son before He was obedient! We believe from a place of belonging and realizing our value. Consider *"the things which He suffered"* in the preceding text. Firstly Jesus *"suffered"* His immortality thus enabling Him to appear in the second point – a Jew. Jesus was born a Jew, under the law system which is the pinnacle of the wisdom of the serpent in the earth. So with this in mind we can safely assume that the things He suffered was the things of the law. Jesus' faith can be defined as Him not regarding this world as having a voice concerning His identity as He suffered it (gave it up) and embraced what was already His in the Father, His true identity. This is how His faith saves us. Before His *"faith"* we had no other option than to adhere to the wisdom of the serpent.

We see the *"suffer"* phenomena also make its appearance following Paul the apostle's encounter with Jesus. Here Jesus commanded Ananias, a disciple in Damascus, on how he was to deal with Paul.

*"15 But the Lord said unto him, Go thy way: for he is a chosen vessel unto me, to bear my name before the Gentiles, and kings, and the children of Israel: 16 For I will shew him how great things he must **suffer for my name's sake**."*
Acts 9:15-16 KJV

Paul was to suffer or give up on the way he perceived God according to the law. Paul's picture of God was formed by the wisdom of the serpent which was the religion of his day. Paul was to give up on that way of life in relating to God. The wisdom of the serpent had been the *"brand"* of faith at the order of the day. I used to be constantly intrigued as to why God would choose Paul to be an apostle to the gentiles. The reason for this way of thinking was that in my mind, Paul had been compromised or corrupted. Puffed up with a lot of knowledge, knowledge that excluded the true nature of God. You see Paul was an expert on the theology of the serpent. Paul or rather Saul spoke serpent fluently. Paul was so literate in the art of serpent theology that it ignited a religious zeal in him, to eradicate anything that doesn't conform to its ideologies.

Paul was the terror attacker of his day. Right from the word go in Paul's conversion episode we see how God teaches him the important things like humility in the gentlest of manners. I believe Paul was stricken with blindness to show him he had been blind to the things of God all along. This is how I believe God creates darkness or evil. He just shows up and the light or good we had been busy with is proven to be darkness or evil.

Now look at the way God chooses to restore his sight. He sends a lowly, dead-scared, wanted man, a disciple in Damascus by the name of Ananias, not the head bishop of the church of Jerusalem, not chief apostle Peter, no. An insignificant member of society, a disciple, to open Professor/Doctor Paul Phd's eyes. These two were exact opposites of the social spectrum. If this was not a lesson in humility then I don't know what is. But by what we observe in Paul's writings it stuck. He knew something important: *"When I'm weak, He is strong."* It became all the more clear on why God would choose Paul. He had knowledge of the law like no other law preacher – the upside being that he understood it in context. He also notes in his writings that *"....we are not ignorant of his devices"* - meaning the devices of satan. Paul knew what went on in the heads of law preachers. What their next move would be and what he would have done in certain situations had he been in their shoes. All these factors made Paul a mighty tool at the hand of God.

*"4 Though I might also have confidence in the flesh. If any other man thinketh that he hath whereof he might trust in the flesh, I more: 5 **Circumcised** the eighth day, of the **stock of Israel**, of the **tribe of Benjamin**, an **Hebrew of the Hebrews**; as touching the law, **a Pharisee**; 6 Concerning **zeal, persecuting the church**; touching the **righteousness which is in the law, blameless**. 7 But what things were gain to me, **those I counted loss for Christ**. 8 Yea doubtless, and I count all things but loss for the excellency of the knowledge of Christ Jesus my Lord: for whom **I have suffered the loss of all things**, and **do count them but dung**, that I may win Christ, 9 And be found in him, **not having mine own righteousness**, which is of the law, but that **which is through the faith OF Christ**, the righteousness which is of God by faith: 10 That I may know him, and the **power of his resurrection**, and the **fellowship of his sufferings**, being **made conformable unto his death**; 11 If by any means I might attain unto the resurrection of the dead."*
Philippians 4:4-11 KJV

In this piece of scripture we see Paul's credentials and then ultimately his regard towards it. His achievements, his education, his ethnicity and moral values did not go to his head. All of these things comprised of who he had been in this world, but it did not define who he really was. Here we have Paul with everything going for him in the system of this world, disregarding it as his identity and counting it as dung.

Verse nine shows us how the faith of Christ is God's objective concerning us and verse ten, the fellowship of his sufferings indicates our subjective response – applying Jesus' *"brand"* of faith, seals us for immortality – verse eleven. Another example of how he applied Jesus' brand of faith to himself is found in what I call, Paul's confession of faith.

*"I am crucified with Christ: nevertheless I live; yet not I, but Christ liveth in me: and the life which I now **live in the flesh** I live **by the faith of the Son of God**, who loved me, and gave himself for me."*
Galatians 2:20 KJV

Paul realizes that he is stuck in a mortal body but the mortal body and its desires could never define him. Jesus' brand of faith defines him. Jesus' brand of faith is the objective, his original design, being created in God's image and applying that to himself subjectively would result in the *"fellowship of His sufferings"* or rather acquiring the right identity. The fellowship of His sufferings is us acknowledging that Jesus fully identified with our human state as Paul noted in Galatians 2:20, *"I am crucified with Christ...."* or 2 Corinthians 5:14, *".... if one died for all, then all be dead."* His crucifixion was our crucifixion. We tap into that truth and are saved. Putting the appropriate load on the pick-up truck, so to speak. Paul believes in the Father the way Jesus believes the Father. This verse is also pretty much self explanatory in the light of what's been discussed concerning: - *not having mine own righteousness - through the faith of Christ - the power of His resurrection - the fellowship of His sufferings* and *made conformable unto His death* in Philippians 4:9-10.

Do you see the importance of Jesus' brand of faith – His way of relating to the Father. The more we pursue the Father in the face of Jesus, the more we suffer/put off the wisdom of the serpent in our lives. These are things that attempt to have a voice in our lives. Fortunately for us we have the victory in Jesus who is the Author and Finisher of our faith!

How many times have you heard a preacher say: *"Jesus learnt obedience by the things He suffered – if Jesus had suffer to learn obedience, so should you!"* Let alone the fact that this is way out of context, it is also the wisdom of the serpent in practice. We do not muster up an imitation of Jesus' faith in our own strength – we believe on Jesus and in doing that we are automatically counting the things of this world, that wants a voice concerning our identity, as dung.

The woman in the garden – The Man in the wilderness

So where do we find Jesus' brand of faith in practice? Jesus' obedience was agreeing with the Father's opinion about Him and that was His victory over the temptation of the devil in the wilderness. Jesus overcoming the temptation by the devil in the wilderness was Him suffering the opinion or wisdom of the serpent and agreeing with the Father's word concerning Him – the Father's objective. His answer to every temptation was Him agreeing or being obedient or His belief in the Father. He overcame temptation by reciprocating the Father's objective. Even though the temptation the woman fell for in the garden is not word for word the same as Jesus' temptation in the wilderness, it was also wrapped up in an angel of light suit, ready to deceive.

"And when the woman saw that the tree was good for food, and that it was pleasant to the eyes, and a tree to be desired to make one wise...."
Genesis 3:6 KJV

As discussed in the part two, we see what man or rather the woman's response to the temptation of the serpent, should have been based on the finished work. This three-fold temptation can be compared to what the apostle John has to say.

*"For all that is in the world, **the lust of the flesh**, and **the lust of the eyes**, and **the pride of life**, is not of the Father, but is of the world."* 1 John 2:16 KJV

First temptation - the lust of the flesh

... . the woman saw that the tree was good for food

"This I say then, Walk in the Spirit, and ye shall not fulfill the lust of the flesh." Galatians 5:16 KJV

"And they that are Christ's have crucified the flesh with the affections and lusts." Galatians 5:24 KJV

We need not crucify ourselves as we already know. Jesus' death was our death. We simply comply with what He already says about us. In this instance the woman's appropriate response should have been. I have no life of my own. The life I possess is the life God had gifted me with. I find my very being in Him. Very much like the testimony of the trees of righteousness in the garden. Paul's confession is along those same line as he also found his very being in God's opinion about man.

"I am crucified with Christ: nevertheless I live; yet not I, but Christ liveth in me: and the life which I now live in the flesh I live by the faith of the Son of God, who loved me, and gave himself for me." Galatians 2:20 KJV

Second temptation - the lust of the eyes

.... and that it was pleasant to the eyes

Being created free-will agents, we have the ability to become that which we behold. God imprinted this into our design. So when the woman beheld this tree and its fruit, she thought to herself: *"This tree looks good. So if I partake of its fruit, I will look good too!"* Taking this a bit closer to home and more relatable to our experience in this world we have a lot of examples of this. Being discontent causes us to think: *"If I only lived in a house like that, I would be something great."* or *"If I drove a car like that, I would be accepted by society."* This, right here is religion whether you're a christian or not. The wisdom of the serpent is not limited to the church. Having a decent understanding of grace prevents the pitfall of not being content with what you already have. Not being content robs us of our peace. Calm down. The finished work is finished, because He finished it! You and I enjoy the benefit when we simply agree with Him.

Third temptation - the pride of life
    .... *a tree to be desired to make one wise*

Ultimately the serpent promised the woman immortality by means of working religion/the wisdom of the serpent. The outcome would in fact be the exact opposite. Their quality of life would now be directly proportionate to their performance and the ultimate reward would be death or to perish, as John 3:16 states in failing to believe on the Son.

Now take a look as to how the devil tempted Jesus. He approached Jesus the same strategy as the one he used with the woman, nothing new and pretty predictable.
"the lust of the flesh" - Tempts Jesus to turn stones into bread because He was hungry. We know Jesus learnt

obedience by the things He suffered. He suffered the things of the flesh. The flesh never had a voice concerning His identity.

"the lust of the eye" - Tempts Jesus to throw Himself from the Temple roof, so angels could rescue Him (An awesome sight!) To appear as the big guy. Doesn't fit Jesus' humility anyways. He did not come to boss the Father around, He came to reveal the Father.

"the pride of life" - Tempts Jesus to worship him, promising to give Him the kingdoms of the world. (You can be like God) To be like God is immortality. Remember Jesus was mortal at this stage. The devil wants Him to work the wisdom of the serpent to obtain immortality. Something the Father already promised Him.

Jesus fulfilled the type the first Adam presented as He willingly came in after us, His woman. He was presented with our temptation and overcame by being obedient to the Father's word and thus authored the very faith by which we have access to our Father and ultimately leads us to immortality.

The woman (mankind) on the other hand, was consumed by a message that promised the very things which was already at her disposal in God. By adhering to this message of a distant futuristic possibility of eventually becoming *"like"* God on account of her own performance, mankind defied her divine design, thereby forfeiting identity, and was subsequently denied access to the Tree of Life/immortality.

I always believed the woman, or rather mankind's salvation in the garden depended on them eating from the Tree of Life, until I discovered that God grants access to this tree when man displays the same mind as Him. *"He who overcomes"* is he who believes the same as God does.

CHAPTER 12
EVICTED FROM THE GARDEN

I mmortality is conditional in its essence and cannot be called conditional immortality, simply because that would raise the assumption that necessitates the existence of unconditional immortality, which would be the cause for even more confusion. I adhere to the the immortality the Father grants unto the faith of Christ.

Let's take a look at as to how this applied in the garden, or rather man's eviction from that garden.

Nothing we do in our own strength could ever bring about eternal life/immortality/manifestation of the sons of God. It is something we are sealed for when we believe. It's the inheritance of the saints. God grants immortality to the right belief-mindset as we have already established. So if He then gave immortality to a guilt ridden, condemned person, as in the case with fallen man in the garden, that would unfortunately result in that individual experiencing utter hell. This person would be stuck for eternity by not having the same conviction God has about him or her.

They would be forever laboring in sorrow to appease a warped version of the Father. The God that does that would most certainly condone a doctrine like eternal conscious torment, which would be contradictory to the nature of immortality, which is in fact conditional.

"And the LORD God said, Behold, the man is become as one of us, to know good and evil: and now, lest he put forth his hand, and take also of the tree of life, and eat, and live for ever:"
Genesis 3:22 KJV

The terms of the law

I view the following scenario as God laying down the rules on how things would now happen, outside of His influence. Away from the garden of influence – and even further away from immortality!

The serpent.

"14 And the LORD God said unto the serpent, Because thou hast done this, thou art cursed above all cattle, and above every beast of the field; upon thy belly shalt thou go, and dust shalt thou eat all the days of thy life:15 And I will put enmity between thee and the woman, and between thy seed and her seed; it shall bruise thy head, and thou shalt bruise his heel."
Genesis 3:14-15 KJV

The serpent is the law preacher or advocate to the tree of knowledge of good and evil that comes in the appearance of the real thing. A deceiver. An angel of light.

"....upon thy belly thou shalt go." This indicates God's

high esteem of the serpent's office and His high regard for his message. *(sarcasm)*

"....and dust shalt thou eat" He will feed on dust death of man (for dust thou art, and to dust shalt thou return Gen 3:19) His seed would be making a living from the sorrowful labor of man, subject to the system that produces death. See *"the seed of the serpent."*

"And I will put enmity between thee and the woman, and between thy seed and her seed; it shall bruise thy head, and thou shalt bruise his heel." Genesis 3:15 KJV

By putting enmity between the woman and the serpent, God makes a distinction between the woman (the victim) and the serpent (the system.) He does not treat them equally but He still gives mankind the desires of his heart, but an emptiness in his soul.

By giving the law, He gives man what he chooses but the reward isn't what He ultimately wanted for His children. He cannot choose on your behalf. The enmity between the seed of the woman (Jesus) and the seed of the serpent indicates that the wisdom of the serpent and the faith of Christ is simply irreconcilable like oil and water, different as night and day.

The seed of the serpent would oppose *"the Faith"* and subsequently have Him executed – bruise His heel. In the very same action *"the Faith"* would prevail, putting to death the old Adam and the monster version of God and crush the serpent's head. Ending the system that brought death to God's people by providing an alternative way of relating to God.

An alternative way in the sense that man is still an agent of free-will. Man still has the choice whether to perform or to adhere to *"the Faith."*

The woman.

"Unto the woman he said, I will greatly multiply thy sorrow and thy conception; in sorrow thou shalt bring forth children; and thy desire shall be to thy husband, and he shall rule over thee." Genesis 3:16 KJV

Subsequent to the fall the woman would be known as Eve - the mother of all living.

"And Adam called his wife's name Eve; because she was the mother of all living." Genesis 3:20 KJV

Eve
H2332 Strong's

חַוָּה

chavvâh
khav-vaw'

Causative from H2331; *lifegiver*; *Chavvah* (or Eve), the first woman: - Eve.

The Apostolic Bible Polyglot translates Eve as *"Zoe"* in Greek old testament, meaning *"life."*

Adam Clarke, in his commentary on this scripture, says the bible translators should have stuck with the Septuagint's translation. In his opinion the verse should have read: *"And Adam called his wife's name "Life," because she was the mother of all the living."*

Eve or *"Life"* would now be the standard of all of mankind. This life on death row, brought on by their choice of faith, the wisdom of the serpent, would be the fate of future generations. All of mankind would from that moment, proceed from this fallen standard. Mankind would have no other option in his limited frame of reference, other than the wisdom of the serpent, to relate to the Father. According to Genesis 3:16 this newly acquired life or identity, would be dependent on your personal performance, conceiving and bearing fruit would be in sorrow and full of labor. While fruit came spontaneously to the other *"trees of righteousness"* in the garden, fruit bearing was now dependent on how hard you labored to produce it. In this sad state, God would ultimately be proportionate to your performance. Remember the tree of knowledge of good and evil? We can also see the dynamics o f *"image"* and *"likeness"* or rather the warped image of God *"faith"* and its outcome/death. The likeness of man is mortality - *".... unto dust shalt thou return"* in the following passage.

" 1 This is the book of the generations of Adam. In the day that God created man, in the likeness of God made he him; 2 male and female created he them; and blessed them, and called their name Adam, in the day when they were created. 3 And Adam lived an hundred and thirty years, and begat a son in his own likeness, after his image; and called his name Seth:"
Genesis 5:1-3 KJV

First of all, *"likeness"* in verse one is a wrong translation. It should read image. The original Hebrew corresponds with the word *"image"* that first occurred in Genesis 1:26. Mankind now procreated with a warped image of God and himself, a life deprived of the life of God and in doing that, his offspring would have the same inheritance – death.
".... and thy desire shall be to thy husband, and he shall rule over thee."
In my opinion God was making a slight tweak in the design of man here. Fallen *Life's* desires would ultimately

comprised of the desires of all of mankind, as she was our mother. When He tells the woman that her desire shall be to her husband, He is actually saying that the human design would now be susceptible and inclined to recognize the real thing by a distinctive key. So how would we recognize the real thing, the Messiah? *".... and he shall rule over thee."*

Jesus made it clear that the ruler or lord is the one who serves. God is saying that mankind would always be searching, knowing there's more to life and inherently be on the lookout for a higher power, to come and bring relief to his sorry state. The key to recognizing this *"Messiah"* that is to rule over us, would be found in the servant attitude of God, manifested in Jesus. Rulers in God's economy are known for their outstanding service. Jesus came to serve us, His woman, with His life.

The law in practice

The reason God gave the law, was for man to realize what the alternative to *"the Faith"*-life, would be like in practice. Man was created from dust and we also see that the plant life and animals also proceeded from the earth. Now note the contrast between the following two passages.

"11 And God said, Let the earth bring forth grass, the herb yielding seed, and the fruit tree yielding fruit after his kind, whose seed is in itself, upon the earth: and it was so. 12 And the earth brought forth grass, and herb yielding seed after his kind, and the tree yielding fruit, whose seed was in itself, after his kind: and God saw that it was good." Genesis 1:11-12 KJV

"17 And unto Adam he said, Because thou hast hearkened unto the voice of thy wife, and hast eaten of the tree, of which I commanded thee, saying, Thou shalt not eat of it: cursed is the

ground for thy sake; in sorrow shalt thou eat of it all the days of thy life; 18 Thorns also and thistles shall it bring forth to thee; and thou shalt eat the herb of the field; 19 In the sweat of thy face shalt thou eat bread, till thou return unto the ground; for out of it wast thou taken: for dust thou art, and unto dust shalt thou return." Genesis 3:17-19 KJV

In the first passage, the earth would yield its produce effortlessly and in the second, the produce would be brought about by the sorrowful labor of man. What happened spontaneously in the garden of influence would now happen on account of man's performance. This new *modus operandi,* was the wisdom of the serpent way of relating to God, in practice.

"Therefore the LORD God sent him forth from the garden of Eden, to till the ground from whence he was taken."
Genesis 3:23 KJV

God takes man out of the garden and then provides him with the building blocks of life, for man to recreate what he had seen in the garden, with one exception. It would not happen by man's strenght not God's faith. We should keep in mind that God was not acting out of arrogance or malice. God did this to show man, that everything God created by faith, could never be replicated by the application of the wisdom of the serpent. In my own words God would say the following to Adam:

"Here's the ground from which all the animals and plants sprung forth at My Word. I want you to apply your new found wisdom (the wisdom of the serpent that tells you you are something great outside of Me) and show yourself, not Me, how you would replicate my life. How you would replicate my influence."
Note that God didn't want man to prove anything to Him.

He wanted man to see that without God's faith he could do nothing. I view God's dealings with man here as the law in practice.

"24 Wherefore the law was our schoolmaster to bring us unto Christ, that we might be justified by faith. 25 But after that faith is come, we are no longer under a schoolmaster."
Galatians 3:24-25 KJV

Paul refers to the law as our schoolmaster or tutor. This means the law was given to teach us something. But what? That you cannot do it yourself. Its purpose was to deplete you of your own performance and strength and point you to the only way you would ever make it. Christ by faith. That you cannot attain unto righteousness by the wisdom of the serpent. The law is there to wear us down, to aid us to come to the end of ourselves. Jesus fulfilled the law by *"suffering"* the wisdom of the serpent by obeying/believing the Father. (Hebrews 5:8-9)

The reward of working (law) for your fill would be death/perish in contrast with *"the Faith"* leading to eternal life. The wisdom of the serpent journey would be sorrowful labor and the destination would be death, ceasing to exist. Applying the faith results in our journey in the here and now to be His quality of life and the destination, immortality.

The angels guarding the way to the Tree of Life

"So he drove out the man; and he placed at the east of the garden of Eden Cherubims, and a flaming sword which turned every way, to keep the way of the tree of life." Genesis 3:24 KJV

We know God drove them out because He had man's best interest at heart. If man had eaten from the Tree of Life prior to knowing good and evil, he would have been in a perpetual state of inferiority, fueled by a different *"faith"* concerning God and subsequently about himself.

Both a design and identity mess, that would inevitably end up in dust.

Cherubim are also known as angels. In this case they are custodians or guardians of what is sacred to God. We see their occurrence also at the ark of the covenant. There they guard the Mercy Seat. Angels also mean *messengers* or *pastors* as we see Jesus relay messages to them, the custodians of His church, in the book of Revelation.

The Cherubim in this specific instance are guardians of immortality. They also bear a message. A flaming sword, something you cannot get past unless you yield to it.

(a flaming sword which turned every way)

Let's get to the sword first. The sword is the word. But what word? The word of God concerning Himself. Seeing Him in the right light. When we acquire that, it also reveals the truth about us. That Word is Jesus. As Jesus is, so are you to the Father right now. If you can accept that you are free to pass. But then what is the fire? This fire is the wrath of God that destroys that which kills God's people, but brings comfort and healing to those who yield to it. It cleanses us form the the faith of the wisdom of the serpent.

Every so often I am confronted on social media or private messages concerning my view on the wrath of God. I am met with:

"We can clearly see God's wrath is exercised against the ungodliness of men!"

This is taken and misinterpreted from Romans 1:18. God's wrath is against unrighteousness, the wisdom of the serpent, and not against man. I am constantly confronted with arguments by the likes of:

"If my daughter is attacked and about to get raped by a criminal, I would not hesitate to shoot him."

Keep in mind, this is an argument used to advocate the notion that God's wrath is against people. My answer is usually this: *"Your daughter is the victim, right? So you would have to be a special kind of stupid, to shoot her, the victim, and not the criminal. I mean, would you really want to project this stupidity to my Father?"* [awkward silence]

"1 For, behold, the day cometh, that shall burn as an oven; and all the proud, yea, and all that do wickedly, shall be stubble: and the day that cometh shall burn them up, saith the LORD of hosts, that it shall leave them neither root nor branch. 2 But unto you that fear my name shall the Sun of righteousness arise with healing in his wings; and ye shall go forth, and grow up as calves of the stall." Malachi 4:1-2 KJV

The Gospel of Jesus is wrath on wisdom of the serpent, *"…. that shall burn as an oven; and all the proud"*, as we see it burns it to stubble, but that very same fire is healing to mankind *"…. the Sun of righteousness arise with healing in his wings."*

The message these Cherubim are wielding to anyone who approaches is this gospel, the *"Faith"* of Jesus. This message is not one that tells you how to get clean. This message cleanses you. How does a message cleanse you? You might ask. It is quite simple - It tells you you are already clean. This is the message declaring your innocence to you and not demanding it. If you wish to pass you need to agree with it, or else you'll stay outside. An inferiority complex brought on by the wisdom of the serpent cannot inherit immortality. God would rather have you return to dust than have you endure eternal torture. (hell)

"3 Now ye are clean through the word which I have spoken unto you. 4 Abide in me, and I in you. As the branch cannot bear fruit of itself, except it abide in the vine; no more can ye, except ye abide in me." John 15:3-4 KJV

My translation of verse three would read: *"You are clean because I say so!"* In John 15 we see Jesus likens being placed in Him, to branches being grafted into a vine. His objective is that we are in Him as He included us in Himself at His death, burial, resurrection and ascension.

Our subjective participation is to abide, to agree, to believe just that, and we would bear His fruit effortlessly. The incarnation of Jesus puts God's objective (our design) on display. When we then acknowledge our design subjectively, we acquire His identity. This identity has an inheritance – the hope of glory!

The way to immortality is guarded by a message. That message reads: *"You are loved, innocent, forgiven and blameless!"* Now that's the good news …. believe it! God grants eternal life/immortality to the man who agrees with His opinion of him. I am reminded of the following scripture:

"Can two walk together, except they be agreed?"
Amos 3:3 KJV

We are spared a lot of bad doctrine and sorrowful labor, when we adhere to the telling of the gospel as told in the garden of His delight. Applying the relationship dynamics that exists within the Trinity, we see the incarnate Jesus as the key to understanding scripture. The garden then becomes the blue-print of God's plan with mankind, when interpreted from the platform of grace.

Allow the Man in the Trinity to influence you with His fullness!   - Grace and peace!

Made in the USA
Columbia, SC
07 December 2018